ESL
Oral Language Practice
in Content Areas

Easy-to-implement,
Effective Activities for
English Language Learners

Karen Clevidence

Illustrated by Kathryn Marlin

Rigby Best Teachers Press®

An imprint of Rigby®

Dedication

In loving memory of my grandmother, Margaret Morell Van Valkenburg. A published author herself, she would have been delighted by this publication written by her granddaughter.

Special thanks to Michelle Parsons for her contributions to the Plants and Technology units and to Mary Susnis for her support and infinite patience.

–Karen Clevidence

Rigby • Steck-Vaughn

www.HarcourtAchieve.com
1.800.531.5015

Editor: Mary Susnis
Executive Editor: Georgine Cooper
Designer: Biner Design
Design Production Manager: Tom Sjoerdsma
Cover photographer: Sharon Hoogstraten
Interior Illustrator: Kathryn Marlin

09 08 07 06 05 04
10 9 8 7 6 5 4 3 2 1

ISBN 0-7578-6681-6
ESL Oral Language Practice in Content Areas

Printed in the United States of America

Contents

Effective Instruction for English Language Learners

Effective language instruction for English language learners (ELLs) must address the wide range of English language abilities ELLs possess. The Stages of Language Acquisition outlined below breaks down the process of language acquisition into five stages.

Stage 1: Preproduction– Students in the preproduction stage are fairly new to English and not yet comfortable producing English speech.

Stage 2: Early Production– Students in the early production stage are just starting to understand some spoken English and are feeling confident enough to produce a few words of English speech.

Stage 3: Speech Emergence–Students in the speech emergent stage are now understanding much of the spoken English in the world around them. Communication often breaks down, but they can make themselves understood in many situations. Despite evident errors in their speech, speech emergent students partake in everyday social interactions, exchanging greetings, and engaging in conversations; however, academic language is still extremely limited.

> *Having a purpose for language production is key to successful language practice and acquisition.*

Stage 4: Intermediate Fluency–Students in the intermediate fluency stage understand most of the spoken English they encounter. Although their speech is not perfect, communication rarely breaks down. There are few barriers to their participation in the English-speaking world. However, they are still struggling to master academic language and to expand their ability to negotiate the various content areas.

Stage 5: Advanced Fluency–Students in the advanced fluency stage comprehend and speak English almost like native English speakers, making few errors. They participate fully in their English-speaking world. However, they may still be lagging several years behind grade level in their competence in academic language and content area knowledge.

The Stages of Language Acquisition chart on pages 12–13 includes the types of responses typically given by English language learners at different stages of English language acquisition and provides examples of the complexity of the language typically demonstrated at each Stage. This chart can help you determine each student's baseline oral language proficiency so that instruction and practice can be tailored to fit all students' English language abilities.

The speed and facility with which English language learners acquire the language varies from student to student depending on a wide range of factors including: education in his or her primary language, home support, personality, amount of exposure to the English language, opportunities to practice the language, and instructional input. The more these students are exposed to English and provided with opportunities to practice it, the more quickly they will acquire the language needed to be successful academically. Language acquisition is a complex process that occurs over time with great individual variation. This means that a student may move in or out of Stages of Language Acquisition, depending on the situation. By tracking each student's Stage development, we can provide English language learners with the differentiated instruction and practice needed to move forward. Assessments for academic language functions, social language functions, grammar usage, and content area vocabulary are provided in the Appendix.

Beyond tailoring instruction and practice to students' Stages of Language Acquisition, we can further facilitate learning by providing an environment that is conducive to language acquisition. An environment that is conducive to language acquisition...

- encourages oral communication.

- engages children in activities that allow them to construct meaning.

- includes consistent modeling, coaching, and opportunities for reflection.

- is committed to providing an anxiety-free atmosphere.

As educators, it is important to focus on what students do well and then to build on these skills. Allow students to make approximations. The most important function of oral language is communication, so focus on allowing students to communicate their messages—grammar and sentence structure develop with practice.

About This Book

ESL *Oral Language Practice in Content Areas* is designed to enhance your classroom instruction by providing additional academic oral language practice. The activities in this book provide oral language practice embedded in theme-based units. The thematic approach provides English language learners with the opportunity to consolidate content area knowledge while engaging in fun and motivating activities. The themes in this book have been chosen to align with standards for Social Studies and Science (grades 3–5).

ESL *Oral Language Practice in Content Areas* can help your English language learners develop academic language skills. Academic language, often referred to as CALP (Cognitive Academic Language Proficiency), is much different from the informal language that students use at home or with peers. It is the language used in the learning of academic subject matter.

Each unit begins with **Content Area Vocabulary.** The vocabulary listed on this page should be familiar to students before they begin any of the activities in the unit. Knowledge of the Content Area Vocabulary will provide students with the background knowledge needed to engage in meaningful oral language practice.

Many of the activities in each unit revolve around the **Reproducible Scenes.** These scenes, along with content area cards and other hands-on visuals and manipulatives, are at the core of each activity. They provide concrete images that help to create language that is understandable to English language learners. The scenes also provide a focus and meaning for the language task at hand. Each reproducible scene can be photocopied and reassembled to create a large illustration. Cut carefully along the inside border. Then align the art and tape the pages together. You may wish to assemble several sets of each reproducible scene for various activities. You may also consider laminating the scenes so they can be used year after year.

Each unit is comprised of many **Oral Language Activities, Variations,** and **Extensions.** These activities provide students with the opportunity to practice language functions and grammar needed to build CALP. Language functions and grammar points that can be practiced are listed at the beginning of each activity, but the focus is up to you. You need not complete every activity or do them in a specific sequence. Concentrate on the vocabulary, grammar, and language functions that match your students' needs.

> **What are Academic Language Functions?**
>
> Academic language functions refer to the specific communication purposes of the activity. For example, some activities encourage students to use language to describe or inquire. (See the Language Functions Chart on pp. 14–15)

Some activities have one or more **Variations.** Variations are based on the Oral Language Activity that precedes them. The variations allow students to practice different language functions or grammar than what was presented in the Oral Language Activity.

All of the activities are designed to be played in a game-like fashion so that students focus on the task at hand, with the language functions or grammar points occurring naturally. This results in a low-anxiety environment necessary for successful language acquisition. English language learners need to use language functions and grammar points in natural situations so that they may later use them again in academic contexts. The game-like activities in this book provide students the opportunity to use the language functions and related grammar points over and over again without feeling like it's rote practice.

Research suggests that it is helpful to have English language learners reflect on the language they use to perform a certain task–that this helps in truly acquiring the language, allowing them to use it in future academic situations (Chamot & O'Malley, 1994). Many of the activities in this book have a **Follow Up** activity where students reflect on the language they used to perform a meaningful and motivating task.

Many of the activities also include an **Extension.** Research suggests that language used for analytical purposes is more likely to be remembered and used again (Bloom, 1956). The Extension activities in this book allow for students in higher Stages to analyze their language use. Extensions are listed immediately following the main activity, but they can be used with any of the Variations for that activity.

Each unit also includes a **Home-School Connection.** The Home-School Connection helps children practice at home the language functions, grammar, and vocabulary they are learning at school.

Many units also contain a **Home Culture Share.** This activity encourages children to use language to share relevant experiences and home culture information with their classmates.

Note: Each activity is designed to involve learners from as many Stages as possible. Not every activity is appropriate for all Stages of Language Acquisition. Each activity clearly identifies the students that are appropriate to include. Within the description of each activity, you will find information about how students in different Stages are expected to participate and sample language production for each Stage. Most activities require no reading and writing, affording English language learners with limited literacy skills the opportunity to develop CALP. It is appropriate for native English-speaking peers to participate in the activities. They can benefit from the content review while providing a model for English language learners.

How to Use This Book

Remember that successful language practice should always begin with two critical steps:

- Be sure that students are familiar with all the vocabulary they will need to complete the activity.

- Provide a model of the desired outcome.

Providing students with this important input before they begin the activity fosters their ability to complete the task and use language meaningfully.

Use the activities to inform you, either pre- or post- instruction. For example, before beginning instruction on the present continuous tense (see Grammar Definitions and Examples, pp. 16–18), you could engage your English language learners in one of the activities that allow for practicing this tense. For those students who do not use the present continuous tense while engaged in the activity, you can proceed with a lesson. Alternatively, you can engage your learners in an activity designed to practice the present continuous tense after they have received instruction to see if they are using it in a situation where one would naturally do so. You can follow up with a mini-lesson on the present continuous tense for those students who do not use it in the activity. The **Assessment Tools** on pages 162–165 are designed to record information about students' Stage development with language functions, vocabulary, and grammar.

The **Appendix** includes the cards and manipulatives needed for many of the activities. Store the cards in envelopes or resealable plastic bags for future use. Each card has the resource letter in the upper left-hand corner so that you can easily sort the cards back into their original categories once they are cut out.

The **Index** is organized so that you can easily reference themes, language functions, grammar points, or content-related activities for a particular Stage. If you want students to practice using language related to a particular grammar point, look the grammar point up in the index, turn to the related activities, and choose those that best match your curriculum and students' profiles, abilities, and needs.

Research and Theory Questions and Answers

Why Should English Language Learners Practice Academic Language?

Research suggests that academic language is more difficult for English language learners to acquire than social language and that it also takes longer to acquire–up to five to seven years–compared with the two to three years needed for acquiring social language (Cary, 1997).

The activities in this book provide English language learners with opportunities to practice academic language with appropriate comprehension supports. Academic language–one of the cornerstones of academic success–can be acquired more quickly with appropriate practice.

Why Should English Language Learners Practice Academic Language Orally?

Research indicates that language development requires language use (Gibbons, 1991), yet research also shows that teachers tend to do most of the talking (Peregoy and Boyle, 1997). In order for English language learners to develop academic language for their mainstream reading and writing tasks, they need to use it (Peregoy and Boyle, 1997). Language use has also been found to be a key component in conceptual learning (Gibbons, 1991)–an area where English language learners cannot slip while acquiring English!

The activities in this book provide an opportunity for your English language learners to use academic language so that they actually acquire it. Such acquisition will allow for greater success in the mainstream classroom.

Why Should Oral Language Practice Be Embedded in Thematic Units?

Many English language learners are expected to learn content, such as science and social studies in their second language. Research tells us that students best learn academic language through meaningful experiences with it. By weaving engaging language practice activities into content area themes, teachers can...

- motivate students to acquire and produce academic language through interesting topics.
- build on background knowledge.
- model language structure and vocabulary needed to communicate about a particular topic.
- include contextualized language use as opposed to isolated practice.
- present opportunities for students to reuse and recycle the vocabulary and content they are learning.

Why Should the Activities Involve Pictures and Manipulatives?

Research indicates that a low-anxiety environment fosters language acquisition (Peregoy and Boyle, 1997). By putting the focus on the pictures and the manipulatives and taking it off of the language required to discuss them, you can create a low-anxiety environment in which your students can acquire language. The pictures and manipulatives also provide comprehensible input, context, and a communication focus—all critical to academic language acquisition (Cary, 1997).

Why Should Academic Language Be Practiced in Groups and Pairs?

Having English language learners work in pairs and groups provides them with an environment where their language production has a purpose—to inquire, negotiate, inform, and so on. Having a purpose for language production is key to successful language practice and acquisition. The activities in this book center around pair, group, and follow-up class-sharing activities.

Why Should Lower Stage Students Be Grouped with Higher Stage students?

Research indicates that peers are a powerful source of language input (Gibbons, 1991). The activities in this book afford lower Stage students the opportunity to receive language input from their higher Stage peers. They further allow for lower Stage students to participate by responding to prompts and commands with gestures, such as pointing, placing and/or moving items, thus receiving language input (acquiring language) in a meaningful context. Such situations also keep students' inhibitions low—one of the keys for successful language acquisition.

Why Should English Language Learners Engage in "Information Gap" Activities?

Research shows that activities that are meaningful and motivating (Gibbons, 1991) are those that will foster true language acquisition. Information Gap activities are meaningful and motivating—they are activities where one student (or several) knows something that another one (or others) does not. The other student needs the information that the one student has to accomplish his or her given task. Such activities give language production a purpose, making English language learners want to use language because they have a motivating task to accomplish. Many of the activities in this book have some element of information gap to them, making your English language learners' speech production motivating and meaningful—a key to successful English language acquisition and ultimate success in the mainstream classroom!

Stages of Language Acquisition Chart

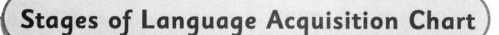

Stage 1: Preproduction *Beginning*	Stage 2: Early Production *Beginning*	Stage 3: Speech Emergence *Intermediate*
• **Comprehension:** Understands little of everyday English. • **Message:** Communicates primarily through gestures or single-word utterances. Able to communicate only the most rudimentary needs. • **Fluency and Sentence Structure:** Produces little, if any, spoken English.	• **Comprehension:** Understands some social conversation but limited academic conversation. • **Message:** Uses routine expressions to convey basic needs and ideas. To some extent, continues to rely on gestures to communicate. • **Fluency and Sentence Structure:** Uses some basic words and simple phrases. • **Word Choice and Academic Language:** Relies on routine language expressions. May use some academic words in isolation.	• **Comprehension:** Understands most of what is said in social and academic conversation but exhibits occasional lack of understanding. • **Message:** Participates in everyday conversations about familiar topics. Although speech contains errors that sometimes hinder communication, student can often convey his or her basic message. • **Fluency and Sentence Structure:** Produces longer, complete phrases and some sentences. • **Word Choice and Academic Language:** Relies on high-frequency words and sometimes cannot fully communicate ideas due to a lack of sufficient vocabulary. Uses some academic language although not always successfully.

Stage 4: Intermediate Fluency *Advanced*	Stage 5: Advanced Fluency *Advanced*
• **Comprehension:** Rarely experiences a lack of understanding in social and academic situations.	• **Comprehension:** Understands social and academic conversation without difficulty.
• **Message:** Engages in ordinary conversation. Although errors may be present, they generally do not hinder communication. Successfully communicates most ideas to others.	• **Message:** Uses English successfully to convey his or her ideas to others.
• **Fluency and Sentence Structure:** Engages in ordinary conversation with some complex sentences. Errors no longer hinder communication.	• **Fluency and Sentence Structure:** Speech appears to be fluent and effortless, approximating that of native-speaking peers.
• **Word Choice and Academic Language:** Range of vocabulary and academic language allows child to communicate well on everyday topics. Begins to use idioms. Occasionally uses inappropriate terms and/or must rephrase to work around unknown vocabulary.	• **Word Choice and Academic Language:** Use of vocabulary, academic language, and idioms approximates that of native-speaking peers.

Language Functions Chart

Academic Function	Definition
Analyze	separate whole into parts; identify relationships and patterns; identify cause and effect; interpret important events and ideas
Classify	group objects or ideas according to their characteristics
Compare (and contrast)	describe similarity and/or differences in objects or ideas or between print, visual, and electronic media
Describe	name; describe immediate surroundings; give an account of an event/action, object, person, and/or characteristics in words
Evaluate	assess and verify the worth of an object, idea, or decision
Explain	express an understanding of a process, an event, or ideas (gleaned from video segments, graphic art, or technology presentations); give the "why" when providing information; ask questions to obtain information or directions
Express position	tell where something is (*here, there, right/left, up/down*); use prepositional phrases of location
Inquire	ask questions to obtain information or directions
Justify and persuade	give reasons for an action, decision, point of view; convince others by clarifying and supporting with evidence, elaborations, and examples
Predict and hypothesize	suggest cause or outcomes
Report	share or recount personal or other factual information
Sequence	put objects, ideas, numbers, or events into a particular order through retelling, role-playing, and/or visually illustrating
Solve problems	define and represent a problem and determine a solution
Synthesize	combine or integrate spoken ideas to form a new whole; summarize orally; draw conclusions from information gathered from multiple sources
Tell time	use words and expressions to express hours and time; talk about calendar

Social Function	Definition
Agree and disagree	express opinion regarding ideas, actions, and so on
Apologize	express remorse for an action or something said
Ask for assistance or permission	use question words to make requests or ask for clarification; request permission; make requests
Express feelings and needs	use words to express emotions, ideas and feelings, refuse
Express likes and dislikes	use words to express likes/dislikes and preferences; express opinions about film, print, and technological presentations with supporting examples
Express obligation	indicate that something should be done to benefit oneself or others, for example, *We should take care of our planet.*
Give instructions	inform or direct a person by telling, explaining, or describing
Greet	use appropriate phrases for welcoming someone, greeting, making introductions, making small talk, such as *How are you? What's new?*; saying and responding to farewell
Negotiate	propose ways of proceeding in group work that recognize the need for compromise and diplomacy
Use appropriate register	vary degree of formality in speech (word choice, diction, and usage) according to setting, occasion, purpose, and audience
Use social etiquette	respond appropriately and courteously to directions and questions; express gratitude; appropriately use polite phrases, such as *please, thank you, excuse me*
Warn	inform of danger; command that someone should or should not do something for safety
Wish and hope	use words to express a desire, such as *I hope I can go to the game; I wish it would snow.*

Some Grammar Definitions and Examples

Grammar Term	Definition	Examples	Some Related Language Functions
Clauses	a group of words that contains a conjunction, a verb and its subject, and is used as part of a sentence	• I put the apples with the grapes **because they are both fruits.** • There are deserts **where my family lives.**	Analyze Classify Evaluate
Comparative	adjectives and adverbs used to compare two things	• There are **fewer** mammals than reptiles in this picture. • The bear is **bigger** than the bird.	Compare and contrast Classify
Coordinating conjunction	*and, but, or, nor* connect words or groups of words	• CDs **and** cassettes • at home **or** at school • Texas is big, **but** New York is small.	Compare and contrast Synthesize
Count nouns	nouns that can be counted	• **peas** • **glasses** of water	Describe Inquire
Demonstrative adjectives and pronouns	words, such as *this/that/these/those* demonstrate what we are referring to	• **This** state is smaller than **that** one. (adjectives) • **This** is smaller than **that**. (pronouns)	Compare and contrast Classify
Future tense	To express actions or situations in the future; formed by using the verb *will* or *is/are going to* plus the main verb.	• The plant in the sun **will be** greener.	Predict and hypothesize Wish and hope
Gerunds	nouns formed by adding –*ing* to a verb	• **Polluting** is harmful to the environment. • They use their wings for **flying.**	Synthesize Explain
Helping verbs	words such as *can, should,* and *must.* They add meaning to the main verb.	• **must** use • **can** fly	Express obligation Negotiate Solve problems Justify and persuade

Grammar Term	Definition	Examples	Some Related Language Functions
Infinitives	verb forms beginning with *to;* can act as adverbs, explaining "why"	• Birds use their wings **to fly**.	Describe Explain
Irregular plural nouns	nouns that do not add *s* to make the plural form	• **geese, sheep, children**	Describe Inquire
Non-count nouns	Nouns that can not be counted	• **water** • **fur**	Describe Inquire
Negative statements	insert *not* between a helping verb and the main verb insert *do, does,* or *did* followed by *not* insert *not* following *is, are, was, were*	• I **will not eat** junk food. • I **do not like** squash. • It **is not** in the forest.	Express likes and dislikes Agree and disagree
Passive verbs	verb form used when the subject of the sentence does not perform the action. Formed by using the verb *be* (in any tense) plus the past participle of main verb.	• A microscope **is used** by scientists. • The leaf **was eaten** by the lizard. • The project **has been delayed.**	Describe Report
Past continuous tense	verb form used to express an ongoing action or situation at a particular time in the past.	• It **was raining** when we drove home. • We **were studying** at 8 o'clock.	Describe Report
Past tense	to express facts or habits in the past; usually formed by adding –*ed.*	• We **designed** a safety device. • We **saw** an eagle.	Report Explain
Possessive adjectives	possessive words that act like adjectives	• **Your** plant is tall.	Compare Classify
Possessive pronouns	possessive words that act like pronouns	• **Ours** has more leaves.	Compare Describe
Prepositional phrases	a group of words beginning with a preposition and usually ending with a noun	• The bird **with the blue feathers** is **in the tree.**	Give instructions Express position

Grammar Term	Definition	Examples	Some Related Language Functions
Present continuous tense	to express an ongoing activity or situation	• The boy **is wearing** a helmet. • They **are wearing** their seat belts.	Report Describe
Present tense	to express facts, truths, and habits	• Bears **sleep** in dens. • He **lives** with his grandmother.	Sequence Explain Express feelings and needs
Present perfect tense	to express an activity within a timeframe that starts in the past and includes the present.	• I **have lived** in the United States for three years. • I **have read** two books so far this month. • We **have been playing** this game since two o'clock.	Describe Explain
Quantity words	words, such as *much* and *many* that express how much; which quantity word to use is based on whether the noun is count or non-count	• My family doesn't each **much** rice. • My family doesn't eat **many** carrots.	Describe
Questions	a helping verb, such as *does, did,* or *are,* is needed to form a question., except when the main verb is one of the following: *is, are, was , were* (see first example).	• Where **is** the squirrel? • What **does** a mouse **eat?** • **Did** you **see** a frog in the pond? • Why **can** a bird **fly**? • **Are** you **going** on the field trip? • **Does** the animal **have** fur? • **Do** you **live** in the desert? • **Did** you **put** the frog card with the amphibians? • **Is** the girl **using** a computer? • **Can** the animal **fly**?	Analyze Inquire Ask for assistance or permission
Superlative	adjectives and adverbs used to compare one thing to all the other things in a group.	• This picture has the **most** mountains. • The elephant is the **largest** land mammal.	Compare and contrast Describe

Land Forms

Content Area Vocabulary

bay	island	pond
canyon	lake	river
coast	mountain	stream
delta	ocean	valley
gulf	peninsula	volcano
harbor	plain	
hill	plateau	

Before beginning, make sure your students are familiar with the content area vocabulary, functions, and grammar points necessary for engaging in each activity. The activities in this unit offer students opportunities to practice language and content for which they have already received instruction. Assess students' participation in the activities and review as needed. Alternatively, you can use the activities to assess students' prior knowledge of the language functions and grammar points before teaching them. The information you collect can be used to guide your instruction.

mountain

timberline

plateau

hill

rocks

hill

canyon

delta

gulf

harbor

island

island

ocean

valley

volcano

tributary

river

hill

rocks

plain

lake

delta

pond

bay

inlet

bay

peninsula

Describe the Picture

Stages: (1)–(2)–(3)–(4)–(5)

Academic Language Function: Describe

Grammar: Present tense sentences with *There is/ There are;* Prepositions–location

Materials: Land Forms Scene

Groups of students describe the Land Forms Scene with as many sentences as they can in three minutes.

- Distribute one copy of the Land Forms Scene to heterogeneous groups of mixed language abilities of three to four students each.

- Encourage students to describe the picture using *There is.../ There are....* Students in Stages 1 and 2 may point to land forms and name them as they are able. Students in lower Stages can also tally the number of sentences produced by their group. Students in Stages 3–5 can include prepositional phrases with sentences, such as *There is a lake next to the mountain.* Students in Stage 3 may say something, such as *lake next mountain.* The group that has generated the most sentences in three minutes wins.

Follow up–Encourage students in higher Stages to reflect on what language they used to describe the scene (*There is.../There are...*).

Stages: (1)–(2)–(3)–(4)–(5)

Variation 1

Academic Language Function: Describe

Grammar: Past tense sentences with *There was/ There were;* Prepositions–location

Materials: Land Forms Scene

Encourage groups to study the Land Forms Scene for a minute or two. Then have them turn the picture over and describe it using sentences, such as *There was an ocean* or *There were mountains* in a game-like fashion as described in *Describe the Picture.*

Draw Your Own Scene

Stages: ①-②-③-④-⑤

Academic Language Functions: Describe, Express position

Grammar: Present tense sentences with *There is/ There are*; Prepositions– location; Demonstrative adjectives/pronouns *this/that* and *these/those*; Subject pronouns *it* and *one*; Contractions (*it's*); Possessives with *'s*

Materials: Drawing paper and markers

Students use self-drawn scenes containing land forms for oral language practice.

- Have students draw their own land forms scene. Do not dictate what land forms they should use nor where they should put them–you'll want variety for language practice. Make sure students put their names on their scenes.

- Gather the class and put all of the students' pictures on a table. Describe one of the pictures without indicating which one you are describing. Use sentences, such as *There is one river* or *There is a mountain next to the harbor.*

- Encourage students to guess which picture you are describing with sentences, such as *I think it's this one* or *It's Nora's picture.* Students in Stages 1 and 2 can participate by pointing to the pictures they think are being described and naming them as they are able with words or phrases, such as *This* or *Nora.*

- Invite students in Stages 3–5 to describe other pictures on the table for their classmates to guess.

Follow up–Encourage students in higher Stages to reflect on what language they used to express position (*in, on, next to, near,* and so on).

Stages: 1 — 2 — 3 — **4** — **5**

Extension

Academic Language Function: Analyze

Grammar: Clauses with *because*; Subject pronoun *one*

Students in higher Stages can explain how they knew which picture was being described with sentences, such as *I knew Marwan was talking about this one because he said there were two mountains.*

Follow up—Encourage students to reflect on what language they used to analyze (sentences with *because*).

Stages: 1 — **2** — **3** — **4** — **5**

Variation 1

Academic Language Function: Inquire

Grammar: Yes/no questions with *Is/Are there...? Is it...? Are they...?*; Affirmative and negative short answers with *Yes, there is. Yes, it is. No, there's not* (or *No, there isn't*). *No it's not* (or *No, it isn't*). *Yes, there are. Yes, it is. No, there aren't* (or *No, there are not*); Prepositions— location

Students guess which picture their classmate has in mind.

- Have students take turns thinking of one student-drawn picture on the table. Then have classmates ask yes/no questions, such as *Are there two mountains?* to guess which picture the student has in mind. Students in Stages 2–3 may use words and simple phrases, such as *two mountain?*

Follow up—Encourage students in higher Stages to reflect on what language they used to inquire (*Is/Are there...? Is it...? Are they...?*).

Home-School Connection

Academic Language Functions: Report, Describe

Students can bring home the picture they drew and describe it to someone at home. They should describe it first in English, and then discuss it in either English or their home language.

Where Are You?

Academic Language Functions: Inquire, Express position, Analyze

Grammar: Yes/no questions with *Are you...?*; Affirmative and negative short answers with *Yes, I am. No, I am (I'm) not;* Prepositions–location; Subject pronouns *I* and *you*

Materials: Land Form Scene
Resource A: People Manipulatives
markers and scissors

Students guess their partner's location in the land forms scene.

- Distribute one copy of the Land Forms Scene and one copy of Resource A: People Manipulatives to each student. Each student also needs markers and scissors. Have students color and cut out a "self" manipulative.

- Arrange students in pairs. Position partners back-to-back so that they cannot look at each other's Land Forms Scene. Students take turns placing their "self" manipulatives in the scene and having their partner ask yes/no questions, such as *Are you on a mountain?* to guess where the student is. Students in Stage 3 may use simple phrases, such as *You on mountain?*

- When the partner thinks he or she knows the student's location, the student shows the partner his or her actual location.

Follow up–Encourage students in higher Stages to reflect on what language they used to inquire (*Are you...?*). They can also reflect on what language they used to express position (*in, on, next to, near,* and so on).

Unit 1: Land Forms

Stages: 1 - 2 - 3 - 4 - 5

Extension

Academic Language Function: Analyze

Grammar: Clauses with *because*

Partners in Stages 4–5 can discuss what helped them or what caused them confusion in knowing the correct location using sentences, such as *I thought you were here because you said to go around the hill, not over it.*

Follow up–Encourage students to reflect on what language they used to analyze (sentences with *because*).

Stages: 1 - 2 - 3 - 4 - 5

Variation 1

Academic Language Function: Inquire

Grammar: Yes/no questions with *Is he/she...? Are they...?*; Affirmative and negative short answers with *Yes, he/she is. No, he/she isn't* (or *he's not/she's not*). *Yes, they are. No, they're not* (or *they aren't*); Prepositions–location

Materials: Land Forms Scene
Resource A: People Manipulatives

In this variation, students guess the location of one or several of the People Manipulatives placed in one location on the Land Forms Scene.

- Students show their partner which People Manipulatives they are placing on the scene and then place the person or people without the partner seeing where they are located.

- In a similar manner as described in *Where Are You?*, partners take turns guessing the locations using yes/no questions, such as *Are they on a mountain?* Students in Stage 3 may use simple phrases, such as *They on mountain?*

Follow up–Encourage students in higher Stages to reflect on what language they used to inquire (*Is he/she...? Are they...?*).

Follow Me

Stages: ①–②–③–④–⑤

Social Language Function: Give instructions

Grammar: Commands; Prepositions–direction, location

Materials: Land Forms Scene
overhead transparency, overhead marker

Students give you directions as you follow them with an overhead marker. This type of activity provides students valuable immediate feedback, as they can see how their directions are perceived.

- Display a transparency of the Land Forms Scene on an overhead projector. Invite students to direct you through the scene using commands, such as *Go around the hill near the large delta.* Students in Stages 2 and 3 can use simple phrases, such as *Go around hill.*

Follow up–Encourage students in higher Stages to reflect on what language they used to give directions (*Go to the.., Head towards,* and so on).

Extension

Stages: ①–②–③–④–⑤

Academic Language Function: Analyze

Grammar: Clauses with *because*

Partners in Stages 4–5 can discuss what helped them or what caused them confusion in giving instructions using sentences, such as *I told you to go over the hill, but I meant for you to go around it.*

Follow up–Encourage these students to reflect on what language they used to analyze (sentences with *because*).

Stages: 1 – 2 – 3 – 4 – 5

Variation 1

Social Language Function: Give instructions

Grammar: Commands; Prepositions– direction, location; Comparative and Superlative

Materials: Land Forms Scene
pencils and erasers

Students follow their partner's directions to draw a path through the Land Forms Scene.

- Each student will need multiple copies (at least two) of the Land Forms Scene. Arrange students in pairs and position them back-to-back so that they cannot see their partner's scene.

- Have students take turns drawing a path through the scene and then directing their partners to take the same path with commands, such as *Go around the hill near the delta* or *Go around the biggest hill.* The partner draws the path based on the students' directions. Students in Stage 3 can give simpler commands, such as *Go hill.*

- When the student is finished giving directions, the partners compare paths.

Follow up–Encourage students in higher Stages to reflect on what language they used to give instructions (*Go...*, *Head towards...*, and so on).

My Favorite Spot

Stages: 1 - 2 - 3 - 4 - 5

Academic Language Functions: Inquire, Report, Explain

Social Language Function: Express likes and dislikes

Grammar: Present tense verbs; Present perfect with *have*; *Wh-* questions

Materials: Land Forms Scene
Resource A: People Manipulatives

Students choose their favorite spot in the Land Forms Scene.

- Each student needs one "self" manipulative from Resource A: People Manipulatives to put in their favorite spot in the Land Forms Scene. Arrange students in heterogeneous groups of mixed language abilities of three to four students each.

- Have students explain to each other why they chose that particular spot with sentences, such as *I love mountains.* Students in Stages 2-3 can explain in simple phrases, such as *like mountain.*

- Encourage higher Stage students in the group to ask follow-up questions, such as *Why do you like mountains?* and *Have you ever been to the mountains? When did you go?* and so on. Students can also state reasons for liking these places using sentences, such as *I like rivers because I can fish in them.*

Follow up–Encourage students in higher Stages to reflect on what language they used to express likes and dislikes (Present tense, such as *I like...*, *Her family lives next to...*, *They go to...*, and so on) and to inquire (*Why...? When...?* and so on).

Stages: 1 - 2 - 3 - 4 - 5

Extension

Academic Language Functions: Report, Explain

Encourage students in higher Stages to conclude the activity by reporting back to the class about their fellow group members' favorite spots with sentences, such as *Carlos likes the ocean because he loves to swim.*

Variation 1

Academic Language Functions: Justify and persuade, Report, Explain

Social Language Function: Express obligation

Grammar: Helping verbs such as, *can* and *should;* Future tense with *will;* Clauses with *because* or *if;* Comparative

Materials: Land Forms Scene
              Resource A: People Manipulatives

Students have three minutes to try to convince as many of their classmates as possible to come to their favorite spot.

- Arrange students into heterogeneous groups of mixed language abilities of four to six students each. Each group must have at least two Stage 4–5 students. Distribute the Land Forms Scene to the Stage 4-5 students in each group.

- Distribute Resource A: People Manipulatives to all students and have each student color and cut out a "self" manipulative.

- Have the Stage 4–5 students in the group place their "self" manipulative on their favorite spot in their Land Forms Scene. Each student must be in a different location. These students should then try to convince the Stage 1–3 group members to come to their favorite spot using language, such as *You will like the river better because you can go swimming here* or *You should come to the mountains because you can relax here.*

- As the other group members are convinced, they move their "self" manipulatives onto that student's Land Form Scene.

- The student that has the most people on his or her scene at the end of three minutes wins.

Follow up–Encourage students in higher Stages to reflect on what language they used to justify and persuade (helping verbs, such as *should* and *can,* clauses with *if* or *because,* comparatives with *better, more* and so on).

Family

Content Area Vocabulary

aunt	granddaughter	mother-in-law
boy	grandfather	nephew
brother	grandma	niece
brother-in-law	grandmother	older
child/children	grandpa	parents
cousin	grandparents	sister
dad	grandson	sister-in-law
father	husband	uncle
father-in-law	male	wife
female	man/men	woman/women
girl	mom	younger
grandchild	mother	

Before beginning, make sure your students are familiar with the content area vocabulary, functions, and grammar points necessary for engaging in each activity. The activities in this unit offer students opportunities to practice language and content for which they have already received instruction. Assess students' participation in the activities and review as needed. Alternatively, you can use the activities to assess students' prior knowledge of the language functions and grammar points before teaching them. The information you collect can be used to guide your instruction.

Rigby Best Teachers Press

Paco   Ana

Eva   Antonio   Dora   Sara

Rebeca   David   Beto

Describe the Family Tree

Stages: 1 - 2 - 3 - 4 - 5

Academic Language Function: Describe

Grammar: Present tense sentences with *This is/ These are*; Possessives with *'s*

Materials: Family Tree, game cube

Students take turns describing the Family Tree.

- Distribute one copy of the Family Tree to heterogeneous groups of mixed language abilities of four to five students each. Also distribute one game cube to each group.

- Have students take turns rolling the game cube onto the picture and describing the person in the tree that the cube lands closest to. Students in Stages 1 and 2 may participate by rolling the game cube and pointing, naming family members as they are able. Students in Stage 3 should use a simple sentence pattern, such as *This is Pilar.* Stages 4-5 students may use possessives with the pattern by saying *This is Anita's aunt* or *These are Tina's parents.*

Follow up–Encourage students in higher Stages to reflect on what language they used to describe (*This is/These are*).

Stages: 1 - 2 - 3 - 4 - 5

Variation 1

Academic Language Function: Describe

Grammar: Possessive with *'s*; Present tense verbs *is* and *are*;

Materials: Family Tree

Students say as much as they can about one person in the family tree using the possessive form.

- Distribute one copy of the Family Tree to heterogeneous groups of mixed language ability of four to five students each.

- Have students take turns rolling the game cube onto the Family Tree. Each student in the group then says something different about the person that the game cube landed on or closest to. For example, one student may say *Eva is Antonio's wife.* The next may say *Eva is Rebeca's mother.* Another can add *Eva is Anita's aunt,* and so on.

- When students run out of things to say about the person, another student rolls the game cube onto the family tree and a different person in the tree is described.

Follow up–Encourage students to reflect on what language they used to decribe connections between family members (possessive with *'s*).

Who's Missing?

Stages: 1 – 2 – **3** – **4** – **5**

Academic Language Functions: Inquire; Describe

Grammar: Questions with *Who*; Possessive with *'s*; Present tense sentences with *He/She is/They are*

Materials: Family Tree

Partners ask and answer questions to fill in their Family Trees. Participating students need to be able to read the labels and approximate their pronunciations.

- Make two copies of the Family Tree. Use correction fluid to mask every other name in one copy. Then mask the other half of the names in the other copy. Do not mask *Anita* in either copy. Label one A and the other B. Make enough copies so that half your students have Family Tree A and the other half have Family Tree B.

- Seat partners back-to-back and distribute Family Tree A to one partner and Family Tree B to the other.

- Partners ask and answer questions to fill in the missing labels on their tree. To begin with, students should ask questions in reference to *Anita* (she should be the only person both Family Trees have in common). For example a student may ask *Who are Anita's cousins?* Their partner may reply *Rebeca and Tina are Anita's cousins.* Students in Stage 3 might ask *Who Anita cousins?* A partner in Stage 3 might reply *Rebeca, Tina* or *Rebeca, Tina cousins Anita.*

- Once partners have filled in their Family Trees, they should compare them.

Follow up–Encourage students in higher Stages to reflect on what language they used to inquire and describe relationships (*Who...?* and Possesives).

Stages: 1 — 2 — 3 — 4 — 5

Extension

Academic Language Function: Analyze

Grammar: Clauses with *because* and *so*

Students in Stages 4–5 can discuss what helped them or caused them confusion in labeling their Family Tree correctly with sentences, such as *I thought you said Mito was Anita's brother, so that's why I put him here.*

Stages: 1 — 2 — 3 — 4 — 5

Who Are You?

Academic Language Function: Inquire

Grammar: Yes/no questions with *Are you...?*; Affirmative and negative short answers with *Yes, I am. No, I'm not;* Contractions with *am;* Possessives with *'s*

Materials: Family Tree
         Resource A: People Manipulatives

Students guess their partner's identity in the Family Tree.

- Distribute one copy of the Family Tree to each student. Each student also needs one copy of Resource A: People Manipulatives. Have students color and cut out a "self" manipulative.

- Arrange students in pairs. Position partners back-to-back so that they cannot look at each other's Family Tree. Students take turns placing their "self" manipulative in the Family Tree over one of the people. Their parnter asks yes/no questions, such as *Are you Rebeca's cousin?* to guess the student's identity. Students in Stage 3 may use simple phrases, such as *You Beto's sister?* Partners may not ask direct yes/no questions, such as *Are you David?*

- Students in Stage 2 should not be expected to ask questions, but may participate by placing the "self" manipulative and answering the yes/no questions about his or her identity.

- Have pairs compare Family Trees when students think they have guessed their partner's identity.

Follow up—Encourage students in higher Stages to reflect on what language they used to inquire (*Are you...?*).

Stages: 1 – 2 – 3 – **4** – **5**

Extension

Academic Language Function: Analyze

Grammar: Clauses with *because;* Compound sentences with *but*

Students in Stages 4–5 can discuss what helped them or what caused them confusion in guessing their partner's identity with sentences, such as *I thought you were Hugo because you said you had one sister, but I see now–David also only has one sister.*

Stages: 1 – 2 – **3** – **4** – **5**

Variation 1

Academic Language Functions: Describe, Inquire

Grammar: Present tense verb *am;* Contractions with *am;* Possessives with *'s;* Coordinating conjunctions *and/but;* Yes/no questions with *Are you...?;* Affirmative and negative short answers with *Yes, I am. No, I'm not.*

Materials: Family Tree
Resource A: People Manipulatives

Students play this game seated back-to-back, placing their "self" manipulatives on the Family Tree as described in *Who Are you?*

- Partners take turns placing their "self" manipulatves and instead of asking questions only, give each other hints, such as *I'm Tina's cousin, but I am not a boy.* Students in Stage 3 may use simple phrases, such as *cousin Alberto.*

- Partners then ask direct yes/no questions, such as *Are you Rebeca?* to guess the student's identity.

- Once a partner has guessed the student's identity, the pair should switch roles.

Follow up–Students in higher Stages can reflect on what language they used to describe themselves (*I am...*).

Stages: ① – ② – ③ – ④ – ⑤

Extension

Academic Language Function: Analyze

Grammar: Clauses with *because*

Students in higher Stages can analyze any successes or misunderstandings that occurred with sentences, such as *I thought you were Anita because you said that Sara is your mother.*

Reconstruct the Family Tree

Stages: ① – ② – ③ – ④ – ⑤

Academic Language Function: Express position

Social Language Functions: Give instructions, Agree and disagree

Grammar: Commands; Affirmative and negative present tense verbs; Prepositions–location

Materials: Family Tree
blank overhead transparency, overhead marker, overhead projector

Students instruct you on labeling the Family Tree as you follow along with an overhead marker. Participating students need to be able to read the labels and approximate their pronunciation.

- To prepare, use correction fluid to mask the names of all family members on one copy of the Family Tree and make a transparency. Display the transparency on an overhead projector.

- Make enough copies of the Family Tree for each student to use as a reference.

- Invite students to instruct you on recreating the Family Tree. You may need to start with prompting questions, such as *Who should I put at the bottom?*

- Do exactly as each student instructs, even if you know it is incorrect. What you write, as well as the other student's input, will provide valuable feedback to the student who is instructing.

- You will revise what you've written as students modify their commands, so you will need something for erasing at hand.

- Stage 2 students' participation may simply be listening and watching.

Follow up–Encourage students in higher Stages to reflect on what language they used to give instructions and to agree and disagree with each other (*Put...; No, she doesn't go...,* and so on).

Stages: 1 – 2 – 3 – 4 – 5

Extension

Academic Language Function: Analyze

Grammar: Clauses with *because*

Encourage students in higher Stages to discuss what caused any misinterpretations in labeling the Family Tree, using sentences, such as *I told you to put Alberto next to Pilar, but I meant on her right side.*

Stages: 1 — 2 — 3 — 4 — 5

Variation 1

Academic Language Function: Express position

Social Language Functions: Give instructions, Agree and disagree

Grammar: Commands; Prepositions–location; *Wh-* questions with *where*

Materials: Family Tree overhead transparency, overhead marker, overhead projector

In this variation, students in Stages 3–5 take turns labeling the Family Tree on the overhead projector, following their classmates' instructions.

Stages: 1 — 2 — 3 — 4 — 5

Variation 2

Academic Language Function: Inquire

Social Language Function: Give instructions

Grammar: *Wh-* and yes/no questions; Affirmative and negative short answers with *Yes, he/she does. No, he/she doesn't. Yes, he/she is. No, he/she isn't* or *he/she's not;* Commands; Helping verb *should*

Materials: Family Tree overhead transparency; overhead marker; overhead projector

In this variation, you and the students take turns asking questions to elicit responses from the class and labeling the Family Tree on an overhead projector.

- Start by taking the first turn yourself to model asking questions, such as *Where should I put Dora? Does Dora have any children?*, and so on, to fill in the tree.

- Students in Stage 3 can use simple phrases, such as *Where Dora? Dora children?*

- The names of the family members will need to be listed on the board or on chart paper. This list will help the student remember who he/she needs to ask questions about.

- Commands should only be given in response to questions.

Follow up–Encourage students in higher Stages to reflect on what language they used to inquire (yes/no and *Wh-* questions).

Group the Family Members

Stages: 1 2 3 4 5

Academic Language Functions: Classify, Describe, Report, Explain

Social Language Functions: Agree and disagree, Negotiate

Grammar: Affirmative and negative present tense verbs; Location words *here/there*

Materials: Family Tree

Students sort the family members according to categories.

- To prepare, make two copies of the Family Tree for each group.

- Arrange students in heterogeneous groups of mixed language abilities of three to four students each.

- Students cut the people (including the name) out of one Family Tree. They can use the complete tree as a reference as they group the family members according to categories, such as mothers/fathers, male/female, and so on, using language, such as *Ana goes with the moms* or *Ana, Clara, Eva, Sara, and Pilar are all moms,* and so on. Students in Stage 3 may use simple phrases, such as *Ana go here.* Students in Stages 1 and 2 may participate by contributing to the sorting, naming items or categories as they are able.

- Students may determine their own categories, or you may provide them.

Stages: 1 — 2 — 3 — **4** — **5**

Extension

Academic Language Function: Report

Grammar: Regular and irregular past tense verbs

Encourage students in higher Stages to report back to the class, explaining the categories they came up with and who they put in each category.

Stages: 1 — 2 — **3** — **4** — **5**

Variation 1

Academic Language Function: Compare and contrast

Grammar: Comparative sentences with *more* and *fewer*

Students sort the family members as described in *Group the Family Members,* comparing and contrasting the sorts with sentences, such as *There are more females than males in the family* or *There are fewer aunts than uncles.* Students in Stage 3 may use phrases, such as *More females.*

Follow up–Encourage students in higher Stages to reflect on what language they used to compare (*more, fewer* and so on).

Stages: **1** — **2** — **3** — **4** — **5**

My Family

Academic Language Functions: Describe, Report, Explain

Grammar: Present tense verbs with *is/are;* Subject pronouns *I, we, he, she, they;* Possessive adjectives *my, our, his, her, their*

Materials: paper and markers

Students draw their own family trees.

- Have students draw family trees of their own families or household members.

● Once the family trees are finished, invite students to share their family trees in heterogeneous groups of mixed language abilities with three to four students each, using sentences such as *This is me. Here is my cousin. He is 12. His dad is Abdul,* and so on. Students in Stages 1 and 2 can point, naming the family members and their relationships as they are able.

Stages: 1 – 2 – 3 – 4 – 5

Extension

Academic Language Function: Report

Grammar: Subject pronouns; Possesive adjectives; Possesives with *'s*

Once all the members of the group have shared their family trees, they should pass them to the person on their left. Students then share their classmate's tree with the class. They might use sentences, such as *This is Afnan's uncle.*

Stages: 1 – 2 – 3 – 4 – 5

Who Is It?

Academic Language Functions: Describe, Inquire

Grammar: Present tense verbs; yes/no questions with *Is it...?, Are you...?;* Affirmative and negative short answers with *Yes, it is. No, it's not* (or *it isn't). Yes, I am. No, I'm not;* Contractions with *is* and *am*

Materials: self-made family trees

You and your students take turns describing the class's family trees.

● Lay all of the family trees onto a table. Start by choosing either all or part of a tree to describe without telling the class what you have chosen. Describe the family tree until someone guesses which one it is. Students can then take turns doing the same.

● Students in lower Stages can point or use simple phrases, such as *Tran family.* Students in Stage 3 can ask simple questions, such as *Is it Tran's family?* or *Is it this?* Students in Stages 4 and 5 should use more advanced structures, such as *Are you describing the tree that Mai made?* or *I think you're describing Mai's family because you said there are three sisters.*

Follow up–Encourage students in higher Stages to reflect on what language they used to describe and inquire (*Are you...? I think you're...*).

Home-School Connection

Academic Language Functions: Report, Explain

Students can bring home the family tree they drew and describe it to someone in the household. They should describe it first in English, and then discuss it in either English or their home language.

Meet My Family

Stages: 1 – 2 – 3 – 4 – 5

Social Language Functions: Greet, Use appropriate register

Grammar: Present tense sentences with *This is*

Materials: Resource A: People Manipulatives
craftsticks, scissors, glue, markers

Students role-play introducing friends to family members.

- Provide each student with one or more copies of Resource A: People Manipulatives. Have them color, cut out, and glue people to craft sticks. They should make enough people to represent members of their household, including themselves.

- Arrange students in heterogeneous groups of mixed language abilities of two to three students each.

- Model using the manipulatives to make and respond to introductions, such as *Mom, this is my friend Anita. Anita, this is my mom.* Mom: *Nice to meet you.* Anita: *Nice to meet you, too.*

- Students in lower Stages can introduce and greet with words or phrases, such as *Mom, Anita. Anita, mom.* Mom: *Hello* Anita: *Hello.*

- Encourage students in higher Stages to use polite language, such as *hello* instead of *hi* when role-playing a child speaking to an adult.

Follow up–Encourage students in higher Stages to reflect on what language they used to greet and be polite (*Nice to meet you.*).

Home Culture Share

Stages: 1 – 2 – 3 – 4 – 5

Academic Language Functions: Report, Explain

Invite students to share with the class how to say family words such as *mother, father, brother,* and so forth, in their home languages.

Describe the Picture

Stages: 1 – 2 – 3 – 4 – 5

Academic Language Function: Describe

Grammar: Present continuous with *are* and *is*

Materials: Family Celebrations Scene

Groups of students describe the Family Celebrations Scene with as many sentences as they can in three minutes.

- Distribute one copy of the Family Celebrations Scene to heterogeneous groups of mixed language abilities with three to four students each.

- Have students describe the picture using the present continuous tense with sentences, such as *They are eating* or *He is singing,* and so on. Students in Stage 3 may use phrases, such as *They eating* or *He singing.* Students in Stages 1 and 2 may simply point, naming the activities as they are able. These students can also be the ones to tally the number of sentences produced by the group.

- The group that has generated the most sentences in three minutes wins.

Follow up–Encourage students in higher Stages to reflect on what language they used to describe ongoing activities (*is* or *are* with an *–ing* verb).

Stages: 1 - 2 - 3 - 4 - 5

Variation 1

Academic Language Function: Describe

Grammar: Past continuous with *was* and *were*

Materials: Family Celebrations Scene

Groups study the Family Celebrations Scene for a minute or two. They then turn the picture over and describe it using the past continuous tense (*They were eating* or *He was singing*). Encourage students to do this in a game-like fashion as described in *Describe the Picture*.

Follow up–Encourage students in higher Stages to reflect on what language they used to describe ongoing activities in the past (*was* or *were* with an *-ing* verb).

Stages: 1 - 2 - 3 - 4 - 5

All in the Family

Academic Language Functions: Describe, Inquire, Report

Grammar: Present tense verbs; Yes/no and *Wh-* questions; Affirmative and negative short answers with *Yes, we do. No we don't*; Prepositions–time; Subject pronouns *I, we, he, she, it, they*

Material: Drawing paper and markers or crayons

Students use self-drawn scenes to describe a family celebration.

- Have students draw a picutre of a gathering for a special event in their family, such as a holiday or birthday. Encourage them to include all the people that usually attend and all the activities that usually occur.

- Once they have drawn their pictures, arrange students in heterogeneous groups of mixed language abilities of three to four students each. Invite students to share their drawing with their group using sentences, such as *My family celebrates Eid. It's a Muslim holiday. It lasts for three days. All the children get gifts and money. We eat lots of good food,* and so on. Students in Stages 2–3 can use phrases, such as *Eid, three day, gift, money.* Students in Stage 1 may show their drawings, naming the event, people, and activities as they are able. Group members should ask follow-up questions, such as *What do you eat? Do you play any games?* and so on.

Follow up–Students in higher Stages can reflect on what language they used to inquire (questions with *wh-* words and *do/does*).

Stages: 1 – 2 – 3 – 4 – 5

Home Culture Share

Academic Language Function: Explain

Social Language Function: Express obligation

Grammar: Helping verbs *should, have to, must;* Adverbs such as *sometimes* and *never*

Students use their pictures of a special event to discuss their home culture's social customs. They can use sentences, such as *You should always take your shoes off when you go into a house,* and so on. Students in lower stages can use phrases, such as *no shoes.*

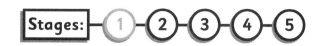

Who Am I Thinking Of?

Stages: 1–2–3–4–5

Academic Language Functions: Inquire, Express position

Grammar: Yes/no questions with *Are you;* Affirmative and negative short answers with *Yes, I am, No, I'm not;* Descriptive adjectives, such as *Asian;* Prepositions–location; Present continuous with *are;* Contractions with *am*

Materials: Family Celebrations Scene

Students guess who their classmate is thinking of in the Family Celebrations Scene.

- Distribute one copy of the Family Celebrations Scene to heterogeneous groups of mixed language abilities of three to four students each.

- Have students take turns imagining they are a person in the scene and allowing classmates to guess who they are thinking of. Classmates should ask questions, such as *Are you cooking? Are you on a couch? Are you Asian?,* and so on to guess who the student is thinking of. Students in Stage 2 can use words, such as *cooking? Man? Asian?* Students in Stage 3 can use phrases, such as *You cooking?* When a classmate thinks he or she knows the person, he or she should say so. If correct, it is his or her turn to imagine being someone in the scene.

Follow up–Encourage students in higher Stages to reflect on what language they used to inquire *(Are you...?).*

Stages: 1–2–3–4–5

Variation 1

Academic Language Function: Describe

Grammar: Present and present continuous tense verbs

Materials: Family Celebrations Scene

In this variation, the student who is imagining him or herself to be someone in the scene should give clues instead of being asked questions.

World and United States Geography

Content Area Vocabulary

boat	hot	south
border	humid	the Southeast
bus	kilometers	the Southwest
car	the Midwest	state
climate	miles	train
cold	north	truck
compass rose	the Northeast	warm
continent	the Northwest	west
country	ocean	the West
dry	plane	
east	region	

Before beginning, make sure your students are familiar with the content area vocabulary, functions, and grammar points necessary for engaging in each activity. The activities in this unit offer students opportunities to practice language and content for which they have already received instruction. Assess students' participation in the activities and review as needed. Alternatively, you can use the activities to assess students' prior knowledge of the language functions and grammar points before teaching them. The information you collect can be used to guide your instruction.

Reproducible: United States Map

Alaska

0   250   500 mi.

0   250   500 km

0   1 in.

0   1   2   3 cm

N
NW   NE
W   E
SW   SE
S

Washington

Oregon

Montana

Idaho

Wyoming

Nevada

Utah

Colorado

California

Arizona

New Mexico

Pacific Ocean

Hawaii

0   150   250 mi.

0   100   200 km

0   1 in.

0   1   2   3 cm

MEXICO

CANADA

North Dakota

South Dakota

Nebraska

Kansas

Oklahoma

Texas

Minnesota

Iowa

Missouri

Arkansas

Louisiana

Wisconsin

Illinois

Michigan

Indiana

Mississippi

Alabama

Ohio

Kentucky

Tennessee

Georgia

New Hampshire

Vermont

Maine

New York

Pennsylvania

West Virginia

Virginia

North Carolina

South Carolina

Massachusetts

Rhode Island

Connecticut

New Jersey

Delaware

Maryland

Florida

Atlantic Ocean

Gulf of Mexico

0	250	500 mi.
0	250	500 km
0	1	2 in.

0 1 2 3 4 5 cm

★ Washington D.C.

Mississippi River

Mountains

ESL Oral Language Practice in Content Areas

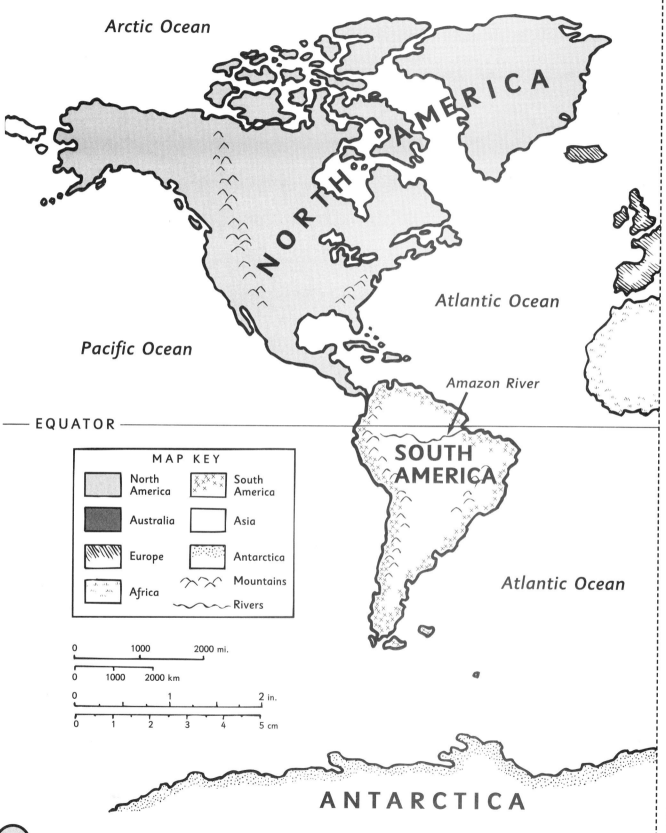

Arctic Ocean

NORTH AMERICA

Atlantic Ocean

Pacific Ocean

Amazon River

EQUATOR

SOUTH AMERICA

MAP KEY

North America

South America

Australia

Asia

Europe

Antarctica

Africa

∧∧∧ Mountains

~~~ Rivers

| 0 | 1000 | 2000 mi. |

| 0 | 1000 | 2000 km |

| 0 | 1 | 2 in. |

| 0 | 1 | 2 | 3 | 4 | 5 cm |

Atlantic Ocean

ANTARCTICA

ASIA

EUROPE

AFRICA

Nile River

Pacific Ocean

Indian Ocean

AUSTRALIA

N
NW   NE
W   E
SW   SE
S

ANTARCTICA

Label the Map

Academic Language Functions: Inquire, Describe, Express position

Social Language Function: Give instructions

Grammar: Prepositions–location; *Wh-* questions with *what, which,* and *where;* Proper nouns

Materials: World Map
United States Map

Note: This activity is best done at the beginning of a unit on world or United States geography, before the students know all the locations of the continents, the oceans, and states. Students will need to be able to read and approximate the pronunciation of the continents or states, and oceans to participate.

Students ask and answer questions of their partner to fill in their maps.

- To prepare for this activity, make two copies of the World Map or two copies of the United States Map. Make two versions of the map, using correction fluid to mask half of the labels on one copy and the other half of the labels on the other copy with the exception of the Atlantic Ocean on the World Map and Texas on the United States Map. Students must begin their questions in reference to one of these locations. Once masked, each map should have labels that the other map does not. Label one map A and the other B and make copies of each.

- Group students in pairs and seat them back-to-back so that they cannot see each other's maps. Distribute map A to one partner and map B to the other partner. Have students take turns asking their partner questions that will help them fill in the missing labels on their maps. For example, one student may ask *What continent is north of Africa* or *What state is west of Missouri?* The other may ask *What ocean is between the United States and Europe?* Or *What state is between California and Utah?,* and so on. Students may not have enough information to answer some questions, but they should continue to ask questions until they get a valid answer. Students in Stage 3 may use simple phrases, such as *What north Africa?* The partner may respond with sentences, such as *Europe is north of Africa.* Partners in Stage 3 may respond with words or phrases, such as *Europe* or *Kansas east Missouri.*

- When the partners have their missing labels filled in, they should compare maps.

Follow up–Encourage students in higher Stages to reflect on what language they used to inquire (Questions with *what, which,* and *where*).

Stages: 1 – 2 – 3 – 4 – 5

Extension

Academic Language Function: Analyze

Grammar: Clauses with *because;* Proper nouns

Students can discuss what helped and hindered them in filling in the labels correctly. They might use sentences, such as *I put Africa here because I thought you said it was south of the United States.*

Stages: 1 – 2 – 3 – 4 – 5

Variation 1

Academic Language Function: Express position

Social Language Function: Give instructions

Grammar: Commands; Prepositions–location; Proper nouns

Materials: World Map
             United States Map

In this variation, instead of asking questions, partners instruct each other on labeling their maps.

- Proceed as described in *Label the Map,* but have partners describe the labeled parts of their maps for their partner to fill in, using commands, such as *Write Missouri on the state east of (to the right of) Kansas.*

Follow up–Encourage students in higher Stages to reflect on what language they used to instruct and express position (commands and prepositions of location).

Stages: ①—②—③—**④**—**⑤**

Extension

Academic Language Function: Analyze

Grammar: Clauses with *because;* Proper nouns

Students in Stages 4–5 can discuss discrepancies and successes using sentences with *because,* such as *I wrote Atlantic Ocean here because you said it was next to the United States, but I thought you meant on the west coast.*

Create a World or United States Map

Stages: ①—②—**③**—**④**—**⑤**

Academic Language Functions: Inquire, Express position

Social Language Function: Give instructions

Grammar: *Wh-* questions with *which* and *what;* Prepositions–location; Commands; Proper nouns

Materials: World Map or United States Map chart paper, rulers

Note: This activity is best done at the beginning of a unit on world or United States geography, before the students know all the locations of the continents or states and oceans. Students will need to be able to read and approximate the pronunciation of the continents or states and oceans to participate.

Students ask and answer questions to construct a world or United States map.

- To prepare, make one copy of the World Map or United States Map for each student. Cut out the states or continents and oceans from half of the copies, keeping each set separate.

- Group students in pairs and seat them back-to-back. Give one partner the cut-out states or continents and oceans along with a large piece of paper to lay them on. Give the other partner the complete map.

- The students with the cut-out pieces need to ask questions of their partner, such as *Where should I put North America?* in order to reconstruct the Map. Students in Stage 3 may use phrases, such as *Where North America?*

- Partners should respond with commands, such as *Put it in the middle of your paper* or *Put it west of Europe.* Partners in lower Stages may use simple phrases, such as *Put middle* or *Put east Asia.*

- Have students compare their maps when they are finished.

Follow up–Encourage students to reflect on what language they used to inquire (Questions with *what* and *which*).

Stages: (1)–(2)–(3)–(4)–(5)

Extension

Academic Language Function: Analyze

Grammar: Clauses with *because;* Proper nouns

Students can discuss any discrepancies and successes using sentences with *because,* such as *I put Atlantic Ocean here because you said it was next to the United States, but I thought you meant on the west coast.*

Follow up–Encourage students to reflect on what language they used to analyze (sentences with *because*).

Stages: ① — ② — ③ — ④ — ⑤

Variation 1

Academic Language Function: Express position

Social Language Function: Give instructions

Grammar: Commands; Prepositions–location; Proper nouns

Materials: World Map or United States Map
paper, rulers

In this variation, proceed as described in *Create a United States or World Map,* but instead of having students ask questions to construct their world or United States maps, have the student with the map intact instruct his or her partner in putting the map together with commands, such as *Put North America to the west of Europe.* Students in Stage 3 may use phrases, such as *North America west of Europe.*

Follow up–Encourage students in higher Stages to reflect on what language they used to give instructions (*Put it...*, prepositions–location).

Stages: ① — ② — ③ — ④ — ⑤

Describe the Map

Academic Language Function: Describe

Grammar: Present tense sentences with *This/That is* and *These/Those are;* Proper nouns

Materials: World Map or United States Map

Groups describe the World or United States Map with as many sentences as they can in three minutes.

- Distribute one copy of the World Map or the United States Map to heterogeneous groups of mixed language abilities of three to four students each.

- Have students describe the picture using sentences, such as *These are states* or *These are continents; This is Texas* or *This is Europe,* and so on. Students in Stage 3 can use phrases, such as *This Texas.* Encourage students in Stages 1 and 2 to point to key geographical areas, naming them as they are able. Students in lower Stages can also tally the number of sentences produced by their group.

● The group that has generated the most sentences in three minutes wins.

Follow up–Encourage students in higher Stages to reflect on what language they used to describe (Sentences with *This/That is...* and *These/Those are...*).

Stages: 1 – 2 – 3 – 4 – 5

Variation 1

Academic Language Function: Describe

Grammar: Past tense sentences with *There was/were;* Proper nouns; Prepositions–location

Materials: World Map or United States Map

Groups study the World or United States Maps for a minute or two, then turn the picture over and describe it using *I saw..., There was/were...* in a game-like fashion as described in *Describe the Map.*

Follow up–Encourage students in higher Stages to reflect on what language they used to describe in the past (sentences with T*here was/were...* or *I saw...*).

Stages: 1 – 2 – 3 – 4 – 5

Variation 2

Academic Language Function: Compare and contrast

Grammar: Compound sentences with *and* or *but;* Adverb *too;* Proper nouns

Materials: World Map or United States Map

Groups describe the map using sentences with *and* or *but,* such as *Rhode Island is small, and New York is, too* or *Texas is big, but New York is not* in a game-like fashion as described in *Describe the Map.* Students in Stage 3 can use simple phrases, such as *Texas big. New York, no.*

Follow up–Encourage students to reflect on what language they used to compare/contrast (compound sentences with *and* or *but* and the adverb *too*).

What Am I Thinking Of?

Stages: 1 — 2 — 3 — 4 — 5

Academic Language Functions: Inquire, Describe, Express position, Compare and contrast

Grammar: Comparative; Yes/no questions with *Is it...?*; Affirmative and negative short answers with *Yes, it is* or *No, it is (it's) not* or *it isn't*; Contractions with *is*; Proper nouns

Materials: World Map or United States Map

You and your students give each other clues about which state, continent, or ocean you are thinking about.

- Set the World Map or the United States Map in a central location where the students and you can see it.

- Take turns choosing a state, continent, or ocean without telling the others what was chosen. Take the first turn yourself to provide a model for the students to follow.

- Students ask yes/no questions to guess the continent, state, or ocean, such as *Is it Colorado?* The student who is thinking of a location responds with hints using the comparative form, such as *No, it's further north* or *No, it's closer to the Pacific Ocean.* Students in Stages 2 and 3 should participate by using simple phrases, such as *California?* or *No, west.*

Follow up–Encourage students in higher Stages to reflect on what language they used to inquire (yes/no questions with *Is it...?*) and compare (*further, closer,* and other comparative forms).

Home-School Connection

Academic Language Function: Report

Students draw their own world or United States maps modeled after the reproducible maps. Students can bring home the map and describe it to someone at home. They should describe it first in English, and then discuss it in either English or their home language.

Where Are You?

Stages: 1 - 2 - 3 - 4 - 5

Academic Language Functions: Inquire, Express position

Grammar: Yes/no questions with *Are you...?*; Affirmative and negative short answers with *Yes, I am. No, I'm not.*; Prepositions–location and description (*with...*); Clauses with *where*; Descriptive adjectives, such as *hot*; Proper nouns

Materials: World Map or United States Map
Resource A: People Manipulatives

Students guess their partner's location on the World Map or United States Map.

- Distribute one copy of the World Map or the United States Map to each student. Each student also needs one copy of Resource A: People Manipulatives. Have students color and cut out a "self" manipulative.

- Arrange students in pairs. Position partners back-to-back so that they cannot look at each other's world or state maps. Students take turns placing themselves on the map and having their partners ask yes/no questions about their location on the map, such as *Are you in the United States?* or *Are you in a place where it is usually hot?* or *Are you in a place with a lot of mountains?* to guess where the student is. Students in Stage 3 may use simple phrases, such as *You in United States?* or *You in place hot?*

● When the partner thinks that he or she knows the student's location, the student shows the partner his or her actual location. Partners then exchange roles.

Follow up–Encourage students in higher Stages to reflect on what language they used to inquire (Yes/no questions with *Are you...*).

Stages: ①–②–③–④–⑤

Extension

Academic Language Function: Analyze

Grammar: Clauses with *because;* Proper nouns

Encourage students to analyze any discrepancies or successes with sentences, such as
I knew you were in Washington because you said you were north of Oregon on the Pacific Ocean.

Stages: ①–②–③–④–⑤

Variation 1

Academic Language Function: Inquire

Grammar: Yes/no questions with *Is he/she...? Are they...?;*
Affirmative and negative short answers with *Yes, he/she is. No, he/she isn't* (or *he's not/she's not*). *Yes, they are. No, they're not* (or *they aren't*);
Contractions with *are* and *is;* Proper nouns

Materials: United States Map
　　　　　　　Resource A: People Manipulatives

In this variation, students place one or several of the people manipulatives in one location on the United States Map. Students should show their partner who they are placing on the map. Partners guess the people's location on the map using the above yes/no question patterns.

Take Me Away

Academic Language Function: Inquire

Social Language Functions: Ask for assistance, Use social etiquette

Grammar: Helping verb *could* to make request; *Wh-* questions with *where*; Helping verb *would like* + infinitive to express desire; Proper nouns

Materials: World Map or United States Map
Resource A: People/Transportation Manipulatives
Resource B: Spinner

Students travel from one place to another as either passenger or driver.

- Distribute one copy of the World Map or the United States Map to pairs. The pairs will also need one copy of Resource A: People/Transportation Manipulatives and one copy of Resource B: Spinner.

- Have students color and cut out their modes of transportation and a "self" manipulative. To use the spinner, students can spin a paper clip around the tip of a pencil.

- Students place their "self" manipulative and one mode of transportation anywhere they choose on the World Map or the United States Map.

- To play, students take turns being the traveler and the driver. The traveler spins the spinner and asks the driver to take him or her in the cardinal direction indicated with a request, such as *Could you please take me east?* Passengers in Stage 2 may simply point or say the direction as they are able. Students in Stage 3 may make their requests with words or phrases, such as *Please east.*

- The driver then asks for further details with a question, such as *Where in the East would you like to go?* Drivers in lower Stages may pose their questions with words or phrases, such as *Where?* The passenger then responds with a request, such as *I would like to go to China, please.* Passengers in lower Stages may make their request by pointing or using words or phrases, such as *Go China.*
  Note: Copy the transportation manipulatives on overhead transparencies. This way students can flip over the manipulative so that it faces the direction in which they want to travel.

- The driver then moves him or herself and the passenger in their chosen mode of transportation to the desired location. Once the trip is complete, the passenger should thank the driver. Students in Stages 2 and 3 may simply say *Thank you*. Stage 2 and 3 drivers should be encouraged to say *You're welcome*. Students in higher Stages should use more complete sentences, such as *Thank you for taking me to Australia* and *You're welcome. I hope you enjoyed the trip.*

- Partners should change roles, mode of transportation, and starting point with each turn.

***Follow up*–**Encourage students in higher Stages to reflect on the language they used to ask for assistance and to use social etiquette (*Could/Would you please...?, Thank you..., You're welcome....*).

Come Here

Stages: 1 — 2 — 3 — 4 — 5

Academic Language Functions: Justify and persuade, Express obligation

Grammar: Helping verbs such as *can and should*; Clauses with *because*; Clauses with *if*; Proper nouns; Future tense with *will*

Materials: World Map or United States Map
Resource A: People Manipulatives

Students have three minutes to try to convince as many of their classmates as possible to come to a particular state or country.

- Arrange students into heterogeneous groups of mixed language abilities of four to six students each. Each group must have at least two Stage 4–5 students. Distribute the World Map or the United States Map to the Stage 4–5 students in each group.

- Distribute Resource A: People Manipulatives to all students and have each student color and cut out a "self" manipulative.

- Have all the Stage 4–5 students in the group place their "self" manipulatives on a region or continent that they think would be nice to visit. They should all be in different places. These students should then try to convince the Stage 1–3 group members to come to their region or continent using language, such as *If you come to California, you can see the Pacific Ocean.*

- As the other group members are convinced, they move their "self" manipulative to the region or continent that they are attracted to the most.

- The Stage 4–5 student that has the most people on his or her chosen state or country in three minutes wins.

Follow up–Encourage students in higher Stages to reflect on what language they used to justify and persuade (helping verbs, such as *should, will,* and *can;* Clauses with *if*).

I Wish

Stages: 1 – 2 – 3 – **4** – **5**

Academic Language Functions: Predict and hypothesize, Explain

Social Language Functions: Wish and hope, Agree and disagree

Grammar: Clauses with *because,* Helping verbs *could* and *would;* Clauses with *if;* Infinitives, Prepositions–location; Affirmative and negative present tense verbs; Proper nouns

Materials: World Map or United States Map
Resource A: People Manipulatives

Students guess where they think their classmates would like to live.

- Make one copy of Resource A: People Manipulatives and the World Map or the United States Map for each student.

- Arrange students in heterogeneous groups of mixed language abilities of three to four students each. Distribute one copy of People Manipulatives and one copy of the World Map or United States Map to each student.

- Have each student color and cut out a "self" manipulative.

- Have students place their "self" manipulative in a place they would like to live. (Have students place open books as barriers so that the other members of the group cannot see what they do with their scene.) Students then take turns predicting and hypothesizing about the locations their classmates have chosen with sentences, such as *I think Enrique chose Minnesota because it's on the Mississippi River, and he loves fishing. If he lived there, he could catch lots of fish.*

- Encourage students to discuss each other's ideas by agreeing and disagreeing with sentences, such as *He may have chosen Minnesota, but I don't think so. I think Enrique chose to live in the Northeast because he loves seafood, and they have lots of seafood there,* and soon.

- Once all of the students in the group have made predictions and hypothesized about where (Enrique) would like to live, (Enrique) should share where he placed his "self" manipulative and his wishes and hopes about living there with sentences, such as *I would like to live in Alaska because I love the cold weather.*

Follow up–Encourage students in higher Stages to reflect on what language they used to express conditional ability and possibility (*If* plus past tense verb, *then...would/could* plus verb).

Home Culture Share/ Home-School Connection

Stages: 1 2 3 4 5

Academic Language Functions: Report, Explain

Grammar: Present perfect verbs; Present tense sentences with *This is*; Possessive pronouns *my, his, her*; Subject pronouns; Proper nouns

Materials: World Map
United States Map
Resource A: People Manipulatives

You and the students share states or countries that you have a connection to, be it a place you have lived, a place where a family member lives, or where your family is from.

- Distribute one copy of the World Map, one copy of the United States Map, and several copies of Resource A: People Manipulatives to each student.

- Model the desired outcome by gluing your self and family manipulatives to states and continents and labeling the people and places. Explain to the class who the people are and where they live, using sentences, such as *This is me in Europe, then in Missouri, and then in California. I have lived in all these places. This is my mom in Europe and Missouri. This is my uncle. He lives in Minnesota,* and so on.

- Send students home with the maps so that family members may help them glue the people manipulatives that represent their family to states and countries.

- Have students share their maps in heterogeneous groups of mixed language abilities with three to four students each. Students in Stage 3 may use phrases, such as *Me Europe, Missouri, California* and so on. Students in Stages 1 and 2 may share their maps, naming the people and places as they are able.

- Group members can share their maps and family members with the class.

- Display the maps around the classroom.

Putting It All Together

Academic Language Functions: Describe, Express position, Evaluate, Inquire, Justify and persuade, Solve problems

Social Language Functions: Express obligation, Agree and disagree, Give instructions, Negotiate

Grammar: *Wh-* and yes/no questions; Location words *here* and *there;* Commands; Affirmative and negative present tense verbs; Proper nouns; Helping verb *should;* Suggestions with *Let's;* Comparative with *-er*

Materials: World Map or United States Map
poster board

Groups of students place the continents or states in their appropriate locations with respect to each other.

- Distribute one copy of the World Map or the United States Map to heterogeneous groups of mixed language abilities with three to four students each. Have students cut out and then recreate the map on poster board or other large format paper by gluing the oceans and continents or states in place.

- Encourage students to use the language functions listed above as they discuss the appropriate location for the oceans and continents or states. For example, one student may start off by asking *Where should we put Florida?* Another student may respond with *Let's put it up here.* The next may say *I think it goes further south,* and so on. Students in lower Stages may participate by pointing to and placing states or continents where they think they go, naming them as they are able. Students can refer to the uncut copies of the World Map or the United States Map if necessary.

Technology

Content Area Vocabulary

airplane	device	remote control
answering machine	doctor	robot
bar code	electricity	satellite dish
bicycle	factory	science
boat	film	space shuttle
bulldozer	game system	stereo
calculator	Internet	tape recorder
camera	invention	thermometer
car	laser	technology
cassette	lawn mower	telescope
cell phone	light	telephone
clothes dryer	machine	television (TV)
CD/CD player	medicine	train
CD ROM	microscope	transportation
communication	microwave	VCR
computer	patent	vacuum cleaner
crane	pencil sharpener	video
DVD	phone number	X-ray

Before beginning, make sure your students are familiar with the content area vocabulary, functions, and grammar points necessary for engaging in each activity. The activities in this unit offer students opportunities to practice language and content for which they have already received instruction. Assess students' participation in the activities and review as needed. Alternatively, you can use the activities to assess students' prior knowledge of the language functions and grammar points before teaching them. The information you collect can be used to guide your instruction.

ANIMAL CLINIC

Describe the Picture

Academic Language Function: Describe

Grammar: Present tense sentences with *There is/are*

Materials: Technology Scene

Groups of students describe the Technology Scene with as many sentences as they can in three minutes.

- Distribute one copy of the Technology Scene to heterogeneous groups of mixed language abilities of four to six students each.

- Have students describe the picture using sentences, such as *There is a computer. There are telephones.* Students in Stage 3 may use phrases, such as *There is computer.* Encourage students in Stages 1 and 2 to point to technology items and name them as they are able. Students in lower Stages can also tally the number of sentences produced by the group. The group that has generated the most sentences in three minutes wins.

Follow up–Encourage students in higher Stages to reflect on what language they used to describe (*There is...There are...*).

Variation 1

Academic Language Function: Describe

Grammar: Past tense sentences with *There was/were*

Groups study the Technology Scene for a minute or two. They then turn it over and describe it using *There was/were...* in a game-like fashion as described in *Describe the Picture.*

Stages: 1 — 2 — 3 — 4 — 5

Variation 2

Academic Language Functions: Describe, Express position

Grammar: Present tense sentences with *There is/are;*
Prepositions–location

Students describe the scene in a game-like fashion as they did in *Describe the Picture,* but they use prepositions of location to express position. For example, students may say *There is a chair next to the computer.* Students in Stage 3 may use phrases, such as *Chair next computer.*

Stages: 1 — 2 — 3 — 4 — 5

Variation 3

Academic Language Functions: Describe, Express position

Grammar: Past tense sentences with *There was/were;*
Prepositions–location

Students turn the scene over as described in Variation 1, but they use prepositions of location to express position. For example, students may say *There was a telescope next to the bed.*

Where Are You?

Academic Language Functions: Inquire, Express position, Analyze

Grammar: Yes/no questions with *Are you...?*; Affirmative and negative short answers with *Yes, I am. No, I am (I'm) not*; Contractions with *am*; Prepositions–location; Subject pronouns *I* and *you*; Location words, such as *inside, outside,* and so on.

Materials: Technology Scene
Resource A: People Manipulatives
markers and scissors

Students guess their partner's location in proximity to a technology item.

- Distribute one copy of the Technology Scene to each student. Each student also needs one copy of Resource A: People Manipulatives. Have students color and cut out a "self" manipulative.

- Arrange students in pairs. Position partners back-to-back so that they cannot look at each other's Technology Scene. Students take turns placing themselves in the scene and having their partner ask yes/no questions, such as *Are you near a computer?* Students in Stage 3 may use simple phrases, such as *You near computer?*

- When the partner thinks he or she knows the student's location, the student shows the partner his or her actual location.

Follow up–Encourage students in higher Stages to reflect on what language they used to inquire (Yes/no questions). They should also reflect on what language they used to express position (*near, next to,* and so on).

Extension

Academic Language Function: Analyze

Grammar: Clauses with *because*

Students in higher Stages can discuss their placements with sentences, such as *I thought you were in the Animal Clinic because you said you were near a computer.*

Follow up–Encourage students to reflect on what language they used to analyze (clauses with *because*).

Stages: 1 – 2 – 3 – 4 – 5

Variation 1

Academic Language Functions: Inquire, Express position

Grammar: Yes/no questions with *Is he/she* or *Are they...?*; Affirmative and negative short answers with *Yes, he/she is. No, he/she is not (isn't/ 's not). Yes, they are. No, they are (they're) not* or *they aren't*; Contractions with *is, are, not*; Prepositions–location

Materials: Technology Scene
Resource A: People Manipulatives
markers and scissors

In this variation, students use one or several of the People Manipulatives in one location on the Technology Scene. Play continues in a game-like fashion as described in *Where Are You?* Partners will need to show each other which person (people) they are placing in the scene.

Stages: 1 – 2 – 3 – 4 – 5

Variation 2

Academic Language Functions: Inquire, Express position

Grammar: Yes/no questions with *Is*; Affirmative and negative short answers with *Yes, he/she is* or *No, she/he is not, isn't,* or *'s not*; Present continuous with *is*

Materials: Technology Scene
Resource A: People Manipulatives

In this variation, students follow their partner's directions in placing all of the People Manipulatives next to a technology item.

- Distribute one copy of the Technology Scene and one copy of Resource A: People Manipulatives to each student. Have students color and cut out all of the people.

- Partners take turns placing all of their people in the scene next to technology items. The student who has not placed his or her people should ask questions about the people's activities to decide where to put them. For example, the partner might ask *Is the boy playing a video game?* Students in Stages 2 and 3 may use phrases, such as *Boy playing game?* or *He playing game?*

- Once the student has placed all of his or her people manipulatives on the scene according to the partner's answers, the pair should compare scenes.

Follow up–Encourage students in higher Stages to reflect on what language they used to inquire (Yes/no questions with *Is*).

Charades

Stages: ①–②–③–④–⑤

Academic Language Function: Describe

Social Language Function: Agree and disagree

Grammar: Present continuous tense; Affirmative and negative present tense verbs

Materials: Resource C: Technology Items

Students use the Technology Items cards to play charades.

- Make one copy of each page of the Resource C: Technology Items and cut them out. Turn the cards over and put them in a stack.

- Bring the class together and have them taking turns picking a Technology Item card without the other class members seeing what it is and acting out using the device. For example, if a student picks *computer,* he or she should act out typing on a keyboard and using a mouse.

- The other class members should guess the activity with sentences, such as *You are using a computer.* Students in Stages 2 and 3 can use phrases, such as *computer* or *using computer.* Classmates who disagree should say so with sentences, such as *I don't think so. I think she's driving a car,* and so on. The first person to guess the activity takes a turn acting out the use of a different Technology Item that he or she picks from the pile.

- Make sure students in Stage 1 have a turn acting out the use of a Technology Item, even if they never guessed a classmate's charade.

Home-School Connection

Academic Language Functions: Report, Describe

Have students color and bring home the Technology Scene and describe it to someone at home. They should describe it first in English, and then discuss it in either English or their home language.

Mix and Match

Stages: 1–2–3–4–5

Academic Language Functions: Describe, Explain, Inquire, Justify and persuade

Social Language Functions: Agree and disagree, Express obligation, Negotiate

Grammar: Affirmative and negative present tense verbs; Passive verbs; Infinitives; Helping verbs *should* and *ought to*

Materials: Resource C: Technology Items
Resource D: Technology Accessories

Student groups match Technology Items to their accessories.

- Make one copy of Resource C: Technology Items and Resource D: Technology Accessories for each group.

- Arrange students into heterogeneous groups of mixed language abilities of three to four students each. Distribute the two resources to each group and have students color and cut out the cards.

- Encourage students to work together on categorizing cards into pairs and/or groups, using sentences, such as (Student 1) *This DVD goes with the game system because you can play DVDs on some game systems.* (Student 2) *Yes, but we could also put it with the computer because you can play DVDs on some computers, so where should we put it?*, and so on. Students in Stages 2 and 3 may use phrases, such as *DVD game system* or *No, DVD computer.* Students in Stage 1 should be encouraged to point to matching cards, naming items as they are able.

- Assure students that it is okay if some cards do not make a match. Encourage groups to create different categories once they have sorted the cards.

- Alternately, you can assign categories for students to sort cards into groups, such as *medicine, transportation,* and *communication.*

What Do I Need?

Stages: ①–②–③–④–⑤

Academic Language Functions: Inquire, Explain

Social Language Functions: Apologize, Ask for assistance or permission

Grammar: Helping verb *can;* Infinitives; Yes/no questions with *Can;* Affirmative and negative short answers with *Yes, I can* or *No, I can not (can't)*

Materials: Resource C: Technology Items
Resource D: Technology Accessories

Students get advice for certain products they wish to use.

- Copy and cut out the cards from Resource D: Technology Accessories and Resource C: Technology Items. Take the following items out of the Technology Items cards (they won't work with this activity): *microscope, thermometer, answering machine, airplane, X-ray, space shuttle, boat,* and *bicycle.* If fewer than twelve students do this activity, give higher Stage students more than one card so that all the cards are used.

- Distribute Technology Items cards to half of the class and Technology Accessories cards to the other half of the class.

- Students circulate around the classroom asking for and giving advice. Students with Technology Accessories cards should initiate the conversations by saying, for example, *I want to listen to this cassette. Can you help me?* Students in Stage 3 can use phrases, such as *Listen cassette. You help?* If the student they have asked has a card that represents a technological device that could be of use, he or she should say, for example, *Yes, I can. You can use my stereo to listen to your cassette* or *You can use my car to listen to your cassette.* "Advisors" in Stage 3 can use phrases, such as *Yes. Use car.* If the student cannot help, he or she should say, for example, *No, I'm sorry. I can't help you. I only have a computer.* Students in Stage 3 can use phrases, such as *No help. Sorry. Computer.*

- Students may consult more than one advisor. They should continue asking other students for advice until you call the group together.

- Once students have had a chance to speak with one or more "advisors," invite students to share with the class the advice they received or gave.

Follow up–Encourage students in higher Stages to reflect on what language they used to ask for and give assistance *(can)*.

Transportation Around Us

Stages: 1 2 3 4 5

Academic Language Functions: Analyze, Classify, Describe, Evaluate, Explain, Inquire, Justify and persuade, Report

Social Language Functions: Agree and disagree, Negotiate

Grammar: Clauses with *because*; Clauses with *where*; Subject pronoun *I*; Helping verb *should*; Yes/no and *wh-* questions; Prepositions–location

Materials: Resource C: Technology Items
large paper bag

Students use student-drawn scenes to decide what Technology Item to put in them.

- Make several copies of Resource C: Technology Items and have students cut out the cards that pertain to transportation (car, airplane, space shuttle, boat, bicycle).

Put the Transportation cards in a paper bag, enough to have one for each student. Allow each student to take a card from the bag.

- Invite students to draw a scene that provides a setting for the transportation card they chose. For example, for space shuttle, a student might draw a picture of space with twinkling stars and Earth in the distance. The pictures should not include the mode of transportation shown on the card.

- Collect the pictures and redistribute them to heterogeneous groups of mixed language abilities of four to six students each. Also give each group several sets of the transportation cards from Resource C: Technology Items.

- Group members work together to identify the missing modes of transportation from the scenes using sentences, such as *What should we put in this scene? I think a space shuttle goes here because it travels in space, and this picture is of space.* Students in Stage 3 can use phrases, such as *space shuttle, space.* Students in Stages 1 and 2 can point to and name the missing Technology Item as they are able.

- Group members should express agreement or disagreement with sentences, such as *Yes (No), I think you're right (wrong).*

- Once group members have placed a transportation card in each scene, they should share one or more of their scenes with the class, explaining their choice.

My Favorite Technology

Stages: 1—2—3—4—5

Academic Language Functions: Explain, Report

Social Language Function: Express likes and dislikes

Grammar: Present tense verbs; Helping verb *can*; Clauses with *because*; Infinitives; Subject pronouns *I, he, she*; Adverbs with *-ly*

Materials: Paper, markers

Students draw themselves using their favorite form of technology.

- Each student needs a sheet of paper and markers to draw a scene of him- or herself using a favorite form of technology.

- Once students have drawn their pictures, arrange them in heterogeneous groups of mixed language abilities of three to four students each.

- Group members should take turns explaining to each other why that form of technology is their favorite and how they use it with sentences, such as *I love computers because I can use them to do my homework more quickly.* Students in Stage 3 can explain in simple phrases, such as *computers good, homework.* Students in Stage 2 can name the technology item they are using in their pictures as they are able.

- Have students share a group member's favorite technology with the class.

Follow up—Encourage students in higher Stages to reflect on what language they used to explain (Clauses with *because*).

Choose Mine

Stages: 1 – 2 – 3 – **4** – **5**

Academic Language Functions: Analyze, Compare and contrast, Describe, Evaluate, Explain, Justify and persuade, Report

Social Language Functions: Agree and Disagree; Express obligation; Negotiate

Grammar: Comparative and superlative with *more than* and *most;* Clauses with *because;* Present tense verbs; Infinitives; Clauses with *if;* Clauses with *then;* Helping verbs *could* and *would;* Affirmative and negative statements

Materials: Resource C: Technology Items

Students debate the importance of two technological items.

Make one copy of Resource C: Technology Items and cut out the cards. Place them in a paper bag.

- Each student takes one Technology Item card from the paper bag.

- These two students should then try to convince the class that the Technology Item on their card is more important than the item the other student has with arguments, such as *An X-ray is more important than a car because you use it to know if you have a broken bone. If you have a broken arm that doesn't get fixed, then you can't drive a car anyway.* The student with the "car" card could then argue the point by saying *Yes, but without a car, you couldn't get to the hospital to have an X-ray taken,* and so on.

- Each pair of students has three minutes to debate their argument. Once the debate is over, students converse and vote on the most convincing argument. Whoever wins the argument gets one point and stays in the game, while a new student comes forward to draw another card and continue the debate.

- The activity continues until all students have had a chance to debate.

- The student that has earned the most points at the end wins.

Health and Fitness

Content Area Vocabulary

apples	doctor	meal	run
badminton	eat	meat	salt and pepper
bananas	eggplant	melon	sit ups
basketball	eggs	milk	skeleton
beans	energy	mouth	skin
beef	exercise	muscles	skull
berries	fat	noodles	soccer
bike	fish	nose	softball
brain	food	nutrients	spinach
bread	fruit	nuts	squash
breathe	football	oil	stomach
cabbage	grains	onions	sweets
candy	grapes	oranges	swim
canoe	green beans	oxygen	taste
carrots	grow	peppers	tornado
cheese	health	picnic	tortilla
chicken	hockey	poultry	vegetables
climb	honey	pork	veins
cook	jump	potatoes	walk
corn	jumping jacks	pull ups	water
crackers	lamb	pulse	yams
cucumber	legs	push ups	yoga
dairy	lettuce	serving	yogurt
dance	mango	rice	
dentist	martial arts	roller blade	

Before beginning, make sure your students are familiar with the content area vocabulary, functions, and grammar points necessary for engaging in each activity. The activities in this unit offer students opportunities to practice language and content for which they have already received instruction. Assess students' participation in the activities and review as needed. Alternatively, you can use the activities to assess students' prior knowledge of the language functions and grammar points before teaching them. The information you collect can be used to guide your instruction.

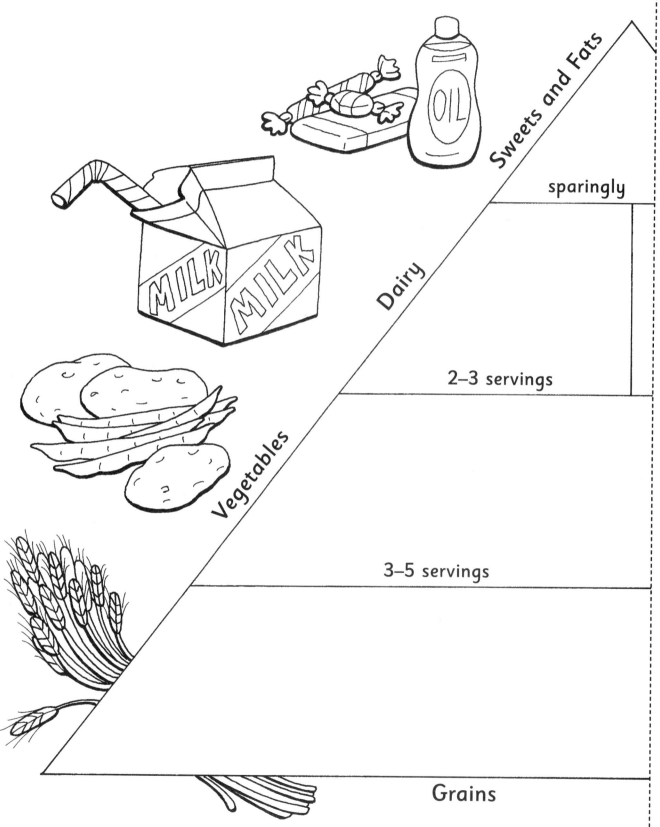

Sweets and Fats

sparingly

Dairy

2–3 servings

Vegetables

3–5 servings

Grains

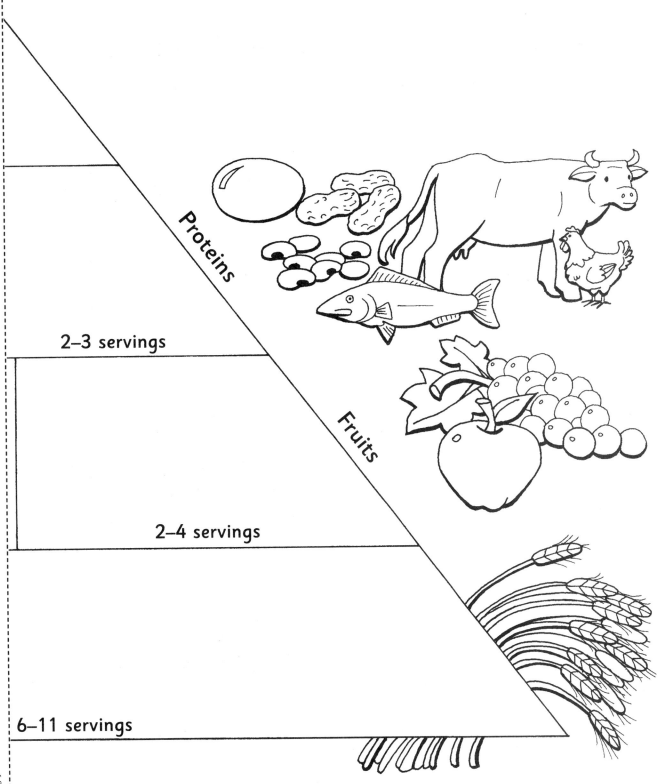

Proteins

2–3 servings

Fruits

2–4 servings

6–11 servings

Sort the Foods

Academic Language Functions: Classify, Describe, Explain, Express position, Inquire, Solve problems

Social Language Functions: Agree and disagree, Express obligation, Give instructions, Negotiate

Grammar: Location words *here/there;* Affirmative and negative present tense verbs; Commands; Clauses with *because; Wh-* questions with *Where* and *What;* Helping verbs *should* and *have to;* Adverb *still;* Suggestion with *Let's...*

Materials: Food Guide Pyramid
Resource E: Foods,
markers, scissors

Groups of students sort Foods cards into the Food Guide Pyramid.

- Make one copy of the Food Guide Pyramid for each group. Make multiple copies of Resource E: Foods for each group.

- Arrange students into heterogeneous groups of mixed language abilities of three to four students each.

- Distribute one copy of the Food Guide Pyramid and several copies of Resource E: Foods to each group. Have students color and cut out the foods. Explain that for this activity each card will represent one serving.

- To play, have groups choose foods to put into each segment of the Food Guide Pyramid so that they have the right number of foods in each group per recommended daily allowances. Students may place multiple copies of the same food in a segment of the pyramid. Students should discuss their placements, making decisions as a group. For example, students can say *Squash goes in "Vegetables"* or *We need one more milk product. Let's put yogurt here.* Students in Stage 3 may use phrases, such as *Squash vegetable.* Students in Stages 1 and 2 can place the foods in the pyramid, naming the food/category as they are able.

- Groups can repeat this activity several times, clearing the foods off the pyramid before starting again. They will have more foods than are the recommended daily allowances for each food group so many combinations are possible.

Follow up–Encourage students in higher Stages to reflect on what language they used to suggest (*Let's*).

Meal Planning

Academic Language Functions: Inquire, Justify and persuade, Report, Solve problems

Social Language Functions: Express likes and dislikes, Agree and disagree, Express obligation, Negotiate

Grammar: Suggestions with *Let's..., Why don't we...?, How about...?;* Adverbs *also* and *too;* Helping verbs *have to, supposed to, should;* Affirmative and negative present tense verbs; *Wh-* questions with *What;* Clauses with *because;* Compound sentences with *but*

Materials: Food Guide Pyramid
Resource E: Foods
Paper (4 sheets per group), glue, markers, scissors

Students plan a day's worth of meals.

- Make one copy of the Food Guide Pyramid for each group. Make several copies of Resource E: Foods for each group.

- Arrange students in heterogeneous groups of mixed language abilities with three to four students each. Distribute one copy of the Food Guide Pyramid and several copies of Resource E: Foods to each group. Have groups color and cut out the foods. Explain that each card represents one serving.

- To play, students choose foods for each meal: breakfast, lunch, and dinner, and foods for a mid-day snack. Together their three meals and snack should satisfy the recommended daily allowances for each food group.

- Group members need to discuss their planning. For example, a student may say *Let's have eggs for breakfast.* Another group member may respond *OK, but let's also have a grain because we're supposed to eat six to eleven servings of grains each day.* Students in

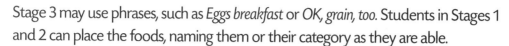

Stage 3 may use phrases, such as *Eggs breakfast* or *OK, grain, too*. Students in Stages 1 and 2 can place the foods, naming them or their category as they are able.

- Once the group members have agreed on their three meals and snack for the day, they may paste the three meals and snack onto four pieces of paper, one for each meal, and one for the snack.

Follow up–Encourage students in higher Stages to reflect on what language they used to express obligation (*should, supposed to,* and so on).

Stages: 1 – 2 – 3 – 4 – 5

Extension

Academic Language Function: Report

Grammar: Past tense verbs; Clauses with *because*

Invite students in Stages 4 and 5 to report back to the class about the meals their group planned.

Follow Your Partner's Directions

Stages: 1 – 2 – 3 – 4 – 5

Academic Language Function: Express position

Social Language Function: Give instructions

Grammar: Commands; Prepositions–location

Materials: Food Guide Pyramid
Resource E: Foods

Pairs of students give each other directions for grouping foods into the Food Guide Pyramid.

- Make a copy of the Food Guide Pyramid and several copies of Resource E: Foods for each student. Cut out the Foods cards from Resource E: Foods ahead of time.

- To play, arrange students in pairs, back-to-back. Give each partner one copy of the Food Guide Pyramid and several copies of Resource E: Foods.

- Have partners take turns grouping foods into the pyramid to satisfy the recommended daily allowance for each food group.

- The student who has arranged the foods should then instruct his or her partner to arrange his or her foods in the same manner, using sentences, such as *Put an onion in Vegetables.* Students in Stage 3 may use phrases, such as *onion vegetable.* Students in Stage 2 can participate by following the instructions.

- When the student is finished instructing his or her partner, the pair should compare pyramids.

Follow up–Encourage students in higher Stages to reflect on what language they used to give instructions (commands).

Stages: 1 – 2 – 3 – **4** – **5**

Extension

Academic Language Function: Analyze

Grammar: Clauses with *because*

Encourage students in Stages 4 and 5 to analyze with a partner any successes or misunderstandings that occurred. They may use sentences, such as *I put the onion here because I thought you said it was a fruit.*

Stages: ① — ② — ③ — ④ — ⑤

Variation 1

Academic Language Functions: Inquire, Describe

Social Language Function: Give instructions

Grammar: Yes/no questions with *Do you have...?*; Affirmative and negative short answers with *Yes, I do. No, I don't.*; Wh- Questions with *Where* and *How many/much;* count and non-count nouns

Materials: Food Guide Pyramid
Resource E: Foods

Students proceed in a similar manner as described in *Follow Your Partner's Directions,* except that the partner asks questions instead of being instructed about where to put the foods. Students should ask questions, such as *Do you have cabbage in your pyramid? How many heads of cabbage do you have? Where should I put it/them?* Students in Stage 3 may use phrases, such as *Cabbage? How many? Where put?*

Stages: ① — ② — ③ — ④ — ⑤

Home Culture Share 🌐

Academic Language Functions: Explain, Inquire, Compare, Describe, Report

Social Language Function: Express likes and dislikes

Grammar: Affirmative and negative present tense verbs; Adverbs such as *often;* Wh- and yes/no questions; Affirmative and negative short answers; Subject pronouns

Materials: Food Guide Pyramid
Resource E: Foods
markers, scissors, paper

Students each make their own food guide pyramid with foods they typically eat at home.

- Make one copy of the Food Guide Pyramid and several copies of Resource E: Foods for each student.

- Distribute the Food Guide Pyramid and Resource E: Foods to each student and have them color and cut out their foods. Students should then arrange on the pyramid only the foods their family eats–enough of each to satisfy the recommended daily allowance. If the foods their family eats are not represented on the cards, they may create some of their own cards to place on the pyramid.

- Once their foods are arranged, have students glue them in place and put their name on their pyramid.

- Arrange students into heterogeneous groups of mixed cultural backgrounds and language abilities of three to four students each. Have students share the foods their family eats with sentences, such as *We eat rice with every meal.* Students in Stages 2 and 3 may simply show their pyramid, naming the foods, categories, and meals as they are able with words or phrases, such as *Rice breakfast, lunch, dinner.* Encourage students to ask follow-up questions, such as *When do you eat yogurt?* or *Do you like eating corn?*

Follow up–Encourage students in higher Stages to reflect on what language they used to inquire (question words and helping verbs, such as *Do/Does*).

Stages: 1 – 2 – 3 – 4 – 5

Extension

Academic Language Function: Report

Grammar: Past and present tense verbs; Clauses with *because*

Invite students in Stages 4 and 5 to report back to the class about a group member's home foods.

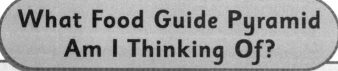

What Food Guide Pyramid Am I Thinking Of?

Stages: ①–②–③–④–⑤

Academic Language Function: Describe

Grammar: Present tense sentences with *There is/are*; Prepositions–location; Count and non-count nouns; Demonstrative adjectives *this* and *that*; Clauses with *because*; Contractions with *is*; Possessives with *'s*

Materials: Student-made food pyramids

You and the students take turns describing a pyramid for the others to guess.

- To play, lay out all of the pyramids the students made in the *Home Culture Share* on page 92. Gather the class around the pyramids.

- Take the first turn yourself, choosing a pyramid to describe without telling the class which one it is. Describe the pyramid with sentences, such as *There are three oranges in the fruits section of the pyramid.*

- Encourage students to guess which pyramid is being described with sentences such as *I think it's this one* (or *I think it's Igor's) because you said there are three oranges.*

- Invite students to describe one of the food pyramids. Students in lower Stages can give hints in phrases, such as *Three oranges.* Students in Stages 1 and 2 can participate by just listening and/or pointing to the pyramid being described.

Follow up–Encourage students in higher Stages to reflect on what language they used to guess (*I think*).

Home-School Connection

Academic Language Functions: Report, Describe

Have students bring home a classmate's pyramid and describe it to someone at home. They should describe it first in English, and then discuss it either in English or their home language.

Exercise

Stages: 1 – 2 – 3 – 4 – 5

Social Language Function: Give instructions

Grammar: Affirmative and negative commands; Contractions with *not*

Materials: Resource F: Exercises
scissors

Students take turns instructing their classmates to do (or not to do) certain exercises in a game-like fashion as in the game *Simon Says*.

- Make one copy of Resource F: Exercises, cut it out, and place the cards upside down in a stack.

- Have students in Stages 4–5 take turns being the leader. The leader should draw a card, instructing the class to do (or not to do) that exercise. For example, the leader may draw "jumping jacks" or "ride a bike" and say *Do (or Don't do) jumping jacks* or *Ride (or Don't ride) a bike.*

- Explain to the class before starting the activity that whoever performs the action when the leader said not to do so is out of the game. Students need to listen carefully for *Do not* or *Don't.*

- Each leader continues drawing cards and instructing the class until there is only one remaining student–the winner for that round.

Follow up–Encourage students in higher Stages to reflect on what language they used to give negative commands (*Do not...* or *Don't*).

What Am I Doing?

Stages: 1 2 3 4 5

Academic Language Function: Describe

Grammar: Present continuous with *You are*

Materials: Resource F: Exercises
scissors

Students play Charades.

- Make enough copies of Resource F: Exercises to have at least one card for each student. Cut out the cards and place them in a pile, face down.

- Students take turns drawing a card and performing the action indicated for their classmates to guess. Students in Stage 1 should not be expected to name the activity, but they can still participate by performing.

- Classmates should guess the activity with sentences, such as *You are riding a bike.* Students in Stages 2 or 3 may use words or phrases, such as *Bike* or *Riding bike.*

- Allow all children the opportunity to act out an activity.

***Follow up*–**Encourage students in higher Stages to reflect on what language they used to describe their classmates ongoing actions (*you + are +* verb with *-ing*).

Stages: 1 2 3 4 5

Variation 1

Academic Language Function: Describe

Grammar: Present continuous with *He/she is...*

Students play Charades as described in *What Am I Doing?,* but instead of describing the action to the person doing it, they describe it to a third party.

- In this variation, have two students go to the front of the room–one to perform the action and the other to address guesses about the action.

- When guessing the action, the students should address the person who is not performing the action with sentences, such as *He is riding a bike.*

Follow up–Encourage students in higher Stages to reflect on what language they used to describe another person's ongoing activity (*He/She* + *is* + verb with –*ing*).

Stages: 1—2—3—4—5

Variation 2

Academic Language Function: Inquire

Grammar: Present continuous tense; Yes/no questions with *Are you...?*; Affirmative and negative short answers with *Yes, I am. No I'm not*; Contractions with *am*

Students play Charades as described in *What Am I Doing?*, but instead of describing what they think the student is doing, they ask that student questions, such as *Are you riding a bike?*

Follow up–Encourage students in higher Stages to reflect on what language they used to inquire about a person's ongoing activity (*Are you* + verb with –*ing*).

Stages: 1—2—3—4—5

Variation 3

Academic Language Function: Inquire

Grammar: Present continuous; Yes/no questions with *Is he/she...?*; Affirmative and negative short answers with *Yes, he/she is. No, he/she isn't* or *he's/she's not*; Contractions with *is* and *not*

Students play Charades as described in Variation 2, but instead of asking questions of the person who is performing the action, they ask questions of a third party.

- In this variation, have two students go to the front of the room–one to perform the action and the other to address questions about the action.

- When guessing the action, the students should address the person who is not performing the action with sentences, such as *Is he riding a bike.*

Follow up–Encourage students in higher Stages to reflect on what language they used to inquire about another person's ongoing activity (*Is he/she* + verb with –*ing*).

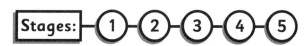

Stages: ①—②—③—④—⑤

Variation 4

Academic Language Function: Describe

Grammar: Past continuous with *You were...*

Students play Charades as described in *What Am I Doing?,* but instead of naming the action while it is ongoing, they wait for the performer to finish, and then guess what the student was doing using sentences, such as *You were riding a bike.*

Follow up–Encourage students in higher Stages to reflect on what language they used to describe a person's past ongoing activity (*you were* + verb with *–ing*).

Stages: ①—②—③—④—⑤

Variation 5

Academic Language Function: Describe

Grammar: Past continuous tense sentences with *He/she was...*

Students play Charades as described in *Variation 4,* but instead of naming the finished action to the person who was performing it, they name it to a third party.

- In this variation, have two students go to the front of the room–one to perform the action and the other to address guesses once the action is completed.

Follow up–Encourage students in higher Stages to reflect on what language they used to describe another person's past ongoing activity (*He/she was* + verb with *–ing*).

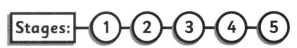

Stages: 1 — 2 — 3 — 4 — 5

Variation 6

Academic Language Function: Inquire

Grammar: Past continuous; Yes/no questions with *Were you...?*; Affirmative and negative short answers with *Yes, I was. No, I wasn't;* Contractions with *not*

Students inquire about the Charades activity as described in *Variation 2,* but they do so using the past tense with questions, such as *Were you riding a bike?*

Follow up–Encourage students in higher Stages to reflect on what language they used to inquire about a person's past ongoing activity (*Were you* + verb with *–ing*).

Stages: 1 — 2 — 3 — 4 — 5

Variation 7

Academic Language Function: Inquire

Grammar: Past continuous; Yes/no questions with *Was he/she...?*; Affirmative and negative short answers with *Yes, he/she was. No he/she wasn't;* Contractions with *not*

Students inquire about the Charades activity as described in *Variation 6,* but they ask questions of a third party.

- In this variation, have two students go to the front of the room, one to perform the activity and the other to address questions about the finished activity.

- When asking about the activity, the students should address the person who is not performing the action with sentences, such as *Was he is riding a bike?*

Follow up–Encourage students in higher Stages to reflect on what language they used to inquire about another person's past ongoing activity (*Was he/she* + verb with *–ing*).

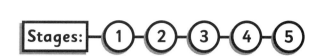

Memory

Academic Language Functions: Describe, Explain, Justify and persuade

Social Language Function: Agree and disagree

Grammar: Demonstrative adjectives/pronouns *This, That, These, Those*; Clauses with *because*; Clauses with *that*; Affirmative and negative present tense verbs; Quantity word *both*

Materials: Resource E: Foods or Resource F: Exercises scissors, markers

Students try to make as many matches as they can.

- Make two copies of Resource E: Foods or Resource F: Exercises for each group.

- Arrange students into heterogeneous groups of mixed language abilities with four to six students each. Have students color and cut out the cards, mix them up, and arrange them face down in even rows.

- Students take turns turning over two cards at a time to see if they have a match.

- As long as the student can persuade the group that his or her match is justifiable, he or she has a match. A match may be two foods in the same food group or two exercises that you do outdoors. Students in higher Stages should use language to persuade the group, such as *These two go together because they are both from the same food group* or *...because they are both exercises that you do outdoors*. Students in Stages 2 and 3 may use words or phrases, such as *same food group* or *outdoors*. Students in Stage 1 may make matches, naming the foods or exercises as they are able.

Follow up –Encourage students in higher Stages to reflect on what language they used to explain their matches (*because* or *both*).

Safety

Content Area Vocabulary

accident	faint	life jacket
adult	first aid kit	oven mitt
ambulance	flashlight	police
blood	flood	radio
bones	hat	rainstorm
break in	heat wave	sandstorm
car accident	helmet	snowstorm
cell phone	help	smoke alarm
earthquake	hurricane	sun screen
electricity	injury	TV
fire extinguisher	jacket	
fire department	knee/elbow pads	

Before beginning, make sure your students are familiar with the content area vocabulary, functions, and grammar points necessary for engaging in each activity. The activities in this unit offer students opportunities to practice language and content for which they have already received instruction. Assess students' participation in the activities and review as needed. Alternatively, you can use the activities to assess students' prior knowledge of the language functions and grammar points before teaching them. The information you collect can be used to guide your instruction.

Rigby Best Teachers Press

Protect Yourself

Stages: 1 — 2 — 3 — 4 — 5

Academic Language Functions: Describe, Express position

Grammar: Present tense sentences with *There is/ There are*; Prepositions–location; count and non-count nouns

Materials: Safety Scene

Students describe the scene with as many sentences as they can in three minutes.

- To play, distribute one copy of the Safety Scene to heterogeneous groups of mixed language abilities with three to four students each.

- Have students describe the scene, focusing on the safety devices shown, using sentences, such as *There is sunscreen at the beach* or *There are bike helmets on their heads.* Encourage students in Stages 1 and 2 to point to the safety devices, naming them as they are able. Students in lower Stages can also tally the number of sentences produced by their group. The group that has generated the most sentences in three minutes wins.

Follow up–Encourage students in higher Stages to reflect on what language they used to express position (*in, on,* and so on).

Stages: 1 — 2 — 3 — 4 — 5

Variation 1

Academic Language Functions: Describe, Express position

Grammar: Past tense sentences with *There was/ There were*; Prepositions–location

Groups study the Safety Scene for a minute or two, then turn the picture over and describe it using *There was.../There were...* in a game-like fashion as described in *Protect Yourself.*

Follow up–Encourage students in higher Stages to reflect on what language they used to describe using the past tense (*There was/There were*).

What Safety Item Am I Thinking Of?

Stages: 1 — 2 — 3 — 4 — 5

Academic Language Function: Inquire

Grammar: Gerunds; Yes/no questions with *Does* and *Is*; Affirmative and negative short answers with *Yes, it does* or *No, it does not (doesn't)* or *Yes, it is* or *No, it is not (it's not* or *it isn't)*; Contractions with *is* and *not*

Materials: Safety Scene

Students guess what safety item their classmate is thinking of.

- Make one copy of the Safety Scene for each group.

- Arrange students in heterogeneous groups of mixed language abilities with four to six students each.

- Have students take turns thinking of a safety device in the scene without telling the other group members what it is.

- The group members then ask questions to guess what the student is thinking. For example, they may ask *Does it keep your hands from being burned?* When a group member thinks he or she knows what the item is, he or she should ask questions, such as *Is it oven mitts?*

- The student who guesses the item first, then takes a turn choosing an item for the others to guess.

Follow up–Encourage students in higher Stages to reflect on what language they used to inquire (yes/no questions with *Does* and *Is*).

Stages: 1 — 2 — 3 — 4 — 5

Variation 1

Academic Language Functions: Describe, Explain

Grammar: Passive verbs; Infinitives; Gerunds

Materials: Safety Scene

Students guess what safety item their classmate is thinking of by using the clues that the classmate gives them.

- Proceed as described in *What Safety Item Am I Thinking Of?*, but instead of having group members ask questions, have the student who is thinking of an item give clues, such as *It is used to keep your head safe*. Students in Stage 3 can give clues in phrases, such as *head safe*. Students in Stage 2 can participate by being guessers, pointing to and naming items as they are able.

Follow up–Encourage students in higher Stages to reflect on what language they used to explain (infinitives and gerunds).

Look Out!

Stages: 1 – 2 – 3 – 4 – 5

Academic Language Functions: Analyze, Explain

Social Language Functions: Warn, Express obligation

Grammar: Helping verbs *should, could, might*; Conditional clauses with *if*; Clauses with *when*

Materials: Resource H: Safety Devices

Students give a group member clues to help him or her guess a particular safety device.

- Cut out enough copies of Resource H: Safety Devices to have one set for each group.

- Arrange students into groups of mixed language abilities with four to six students each. Students should sit in a circle. Give each group a set of Safety Devices cards.

- One student chooses a card without letting the student to the left see it. The student with the card holds it over the student to his or her left so that all the other group members can see it.

- Group members should then give the student with the card over his or her head hints to help him or her guess the Safety Device with sentences, such as *You should use this when you're riding in a car* or *If you don't use this, you might hurt your head*, and so on.

- Group members continue giving hints until the student guesses the safety device. Play then continues around the circle with the student who had been guessing, holding the next card over the student to his or her left.

What Should I Do?

Academic Language Functions: Explain, Report

Social Language Functions: Ask for assistance or permission, Express obligation, Use social etiquette

Grammar: Present tense verbs; Infinitives; Yes/no questions with *Can*; Helping verbs *should, have to, must, had better*; Prepositional phrases with *in case*; Negative sentences with *can not (can't)*; Contractions with *not*

Materials: Resource H: Safety Devices
Resource I: Activities
scissors

Students ask for advice for certain activities they wish to perform.

- Make enough copies of Resource H: Safety Devices for half the number of students in your class, as well as enough copies of Resource I: Activities for half the number of students in your class.

- Cut out the cards and give half the class Safety Devices and the other half Activities.

- Have students circulate around the room asking for and giving advice. Students with activity cards should initiate the conversations by saying, for example, *I want to ride my bike. Can you give me safety advice?* Students in Stage 3 may say *Ride bike. Safety?* Students should show their activity cards as they ask for advice. If the student they have asked has a card that represents a safety device that could be used for that activity, he or she should say *Yes, I can* and then offer advice, such as *You should wear a helmet. It will protect your head.* Students in Stage 3 may respond with *Wear helmet. Protect head.* If the student they have asked does not have a safety device that can help, the student should say *No, I'm sorry. I can't.* Students should continue to seek advice until they have spoken to at least two people who were able to give advice.

Follow up–Encourage students in higher Stages to reflect on what language they used to give advice (Helping verbs *should, have to, must, had better*).

Stages: 1 — 2 — 3 — **4** — **5**

Extension

Academic Language Function: Report

Grammar: Past tense verbs

Invite students in Stages 4 and 5 to report back to the class about the advice that was given or received.

Stages: 1 — 2 — **3** — **4** — **5**

How Does It Work?

Academic Language Functions: Describe, Explain, Synthesize

Social Language Functions: Agree and disagree, Express obligation

Grammar: Affirmative and negative present tense verbs; Helping verbs *should, must, have to;* Clauses with *when;* Gerunds; Prepositions–location

Materials: Safety Scene

Students discuss when a safety device is used, how it helps, and how it works.

- Make enough copies of the Safety Scene for each group of students.

- Arrange students into heterogeneous groups of mixed language abilities with three to four students each. Distribute one copy of the Safety Scene and a game cube or small foil ball to each pair.

- Have students take turns rolling the cube or ball onto the scene and then discussing the safety item that it has landed closest to. The team receives one point for each of the following items they discuss: when and where the item should be used, how it helps, and how it works. For example, they may start their discussion with *A smoke alarm should be in every building. It helps people know when there* is a fire. It needs a fresh battery that you should change every year. It works by making a loud sound when it detects smoke. Students in Stage 3 may use phrases, such as *Use in building. Need battery,* and so on.

Follow up–Encourage students in higher Stages to reflect on what language they used to express obligation (*should, have to, must*).

Where Are You?

Stages: ①–②–③–④–⑤

Academic Language Functions: Inquire, Express position

Grammar: Yes/no questions with *Are you...?*; Affirmative and negative short answers with *Yes, I am. No, I am (I'm) not*; Contractions with *am*; Location words *outside/inside*; Prepositions–location; Present continuous

Materials: Safety Scene
Resource A: People Manipulatives
markers, scissors

Students guess their partner's location in the Safety Scene.

- Distribute one copy of the Safety Scene to each student. Each student also needs one copy of Resource A: People Manipulatives. Have students color and cut out a "self" manipulative.

- To play, arrange students in pairs. Position partners back-to-back so that they cannot look at each other's Safety Scene. Students take turns placing themselves in the scene and having their partner ask yes/no questions, such as *Are you using something to protect your skin?* to guess their partner's activity and location. Students in Stage 3 may use phrases, such as *You outside?*

- When the partner thinks he or she knows the student's location, the student shows the partner his or her actual location.

Follow up–Encourage students in higher Stages to reflect on what language they used to inquire (*Are you...?*). They should also reflect on what language they used to express their activities (present continuous tense–*I am* + verb with *–ing*).

Stages: ① ② ③ ④ ⑤

Extension

Academic Language Function: Analyze

Grammar: Clauses with *because*; Past continuous; Present tense verbs; Infinitives; Compound sentences with *but*

Students can discuss any discrepancies and successes in guessing their partner's activity and location with sentences, such as *I thought you were inside cooking because you said you were using something to protect your skin, but now I see you were outside using sunscreen.*

Stages: ① ② ③ ④ ⑤

Variation 1

Academic Language Function: Inquire, Express position

Grammar: Yes/no questions with *Is he/she...? Are they...?* Affirmative and negative short answers with *Yes, he/she is* or *they are. No, he/she is not (isn't)/he's/she's not* or *they are not (they're not* or *they aren't)*; Contractions with *is, are,* and *not*

In this variation, students place one or several of the People Manipulatives in one location on the scene. Play continues in a game-like fashion as described in *Where Are You?*

● Have students color and cut out one or more of the People Manipulatives to place in the scene.

Stages: ① ② ③ ④ ⑤

Safety Inventions

Academic Language Functions: Explain, Report, Inquire

Grammar: Clauses with *when*; Infinitives; Past tense verbs; Subject pronouns *he* and *she*; Helping verbs *can, should* and *must*; Clauses with *that*; Prepositions–location; *Wh-* questions

Materials: paper, one sheet per student; markers or crayons

Students create their own safety devices.

- Have students draw safety devices of their own creation. They should draw them within the situation/activity they would be used.

- Once students have drawn their inventions, arrange students in heterogeneous groups of mixed language abilities with three to four students each.

- Invite students to take turns sharing their invention with their group using sentences, such as *I designed a device that can help to protect you in a car accident. It's a separate part you sit in. When you have an accident, the part you're sitting in shoots off away from the accident.* Students in Stage 3 can use phrases, such as *Help in car.* Students in Stage 2 can show their invention, naming parts and describing it with words as they are able.

- Encourage group members to ask for further details, such as *What part of the car does it attach to?* Students in Stage 3 can use phrases, such as *Where in car?*

- Invite students to share a group member's inventions with the class.

Safety Procedures

Stages: 1 — 2 — 3 — 4 — 5

Academic Language Functions: Evaluate, Explain, Justify and persuade, Report, Solve problems, Synthesize

Social Language Functions: Agree and disagree, Express obligation, Negotiate

Grammar: Prepositional phrases with *In case of*; Prepositions–location; Helping verb *should*; Gerunds; Adverbs with *-ly*

Materials: Resource G: Emergencies

Students discuss procedures for certain emergency situations.

- Make one copy of Resource G: Emergencies and cut out the cards.

- Arrange students in groups of mixed language abilities with four to six students each. Distribute emergency cards to each group.

- Have groups discuss safety procedures for each emergency situation. For example, if the group has the *Fire* card, they may say *In case of a fire in your home, you should leave the home immediately. Your family should have a plan for leaving the home and meeting outside,* and so forth. Students in Stage 3 may participate with phrases, such as *Fire, leave home.*

- Once groups are finished deciding their safety procedures, they should share their decisions with the class. Contribute knowledge that you have on emergency and safety procedures to the discussion.

Stages: ①—②—③—④—⑤

Variation 1

Academic Language Functions: Classify, Evaluate, Explain, Justify and persuade, Solve problems, Synthesize

Social Language Functions: Agree and disagree, Express obligation, Negotiate

Grammar: Prepostional phrases with *In case of*; Prepositions– location; Helping verb *should;* Gerunds; Helping verbs *would* and *could*; Adverbs *also* and *too.*

Materials: Resource G: Emergencies
Resource H: Safety Devices

Each group has one Emergency card as described in *Safety Procedures,* but they also get a complete set of cards from Resource H: Safety Devices.

- Groups begin by sorting through the Safety Devices cards, choosing those cards which represent devices that might be helpful in their emergency. For example, a student might say *The fire extinguisher could help put out the fire.* Another student might add *It would also be helpful to have a cell phone in case of a fire,* and so on. Students in Stage 3 may use phrases, such as *extinguisher help* or *Cell phone good.* Students in Stages 1 and 2 can pick up helpful Safety Devices cards, naming them as they are able.

Animal Adaptations and Habitats

Content Area Vocabulary

adaptation	feathers	moth	scratch
alligator	feet	mouse/mice	sheep
amphibian	fin	nest	skin
animal	fish	opossum	snake
ant	frog	owl	spider
beak	forest	paddle	spider web
bill	fox	pond	squirrel
bird	fur	predator	stingray
butterfly	goose/geese	protection	survive
camouflage	habitat	pupa	tadpole
caterpillar	insect	raccoon	tail
catfish	lake	reptile	teeth
chicken	larva	river	tree
den	lizard	rock	turtle
duck	log	salamander	walkingstick
egg	mammal	scales	wings

Before beginning, make sure your students are familiar with the content area vocabulary, functions, and grammar points necessary for engaging in each activity. The activities in this unit offer students opportunities to practice language and content for which they have already received instruction. Assess students' participation in the activities and review as needed. Alternatively, you can use the activities to assess students' prior knowledge of the language functions and grammar points before teaching them. The information you collect can be used to guide your instruction.

Animal Facts

Stages: ① — ② — ③ — ④ — ⑤

Academic Language Functions: Describe, Inquire

Grammar: Present tense verbs; Yes/no question with *Am I...? Do I...?*; Affirmative and negative short answers with *Yes, you are. No, you're not* or *you aren't;* Contractions with *are* and *not. Yes, you do. No you don't.*

Materials: Resource J: Animals

Students need to guess the identy of an unknown animal.

- Make enough copies of Resource J: Animals for there to be two or three animals per student. Cut out the animals and tape one animal to each student's back without the student seeing which animal you have taped to his or her back. Some students may have the same animal.

- Students circulate around the room and give each other clues, such as *You live in the forest* or *You are a mammal.* Students guess their animal identity with questions, such as *Am I a frog?* Students in Stages 2 and 3 can give simple clues and guesses in phrases, such as *live forest* and *Frog?* If a student guesses his or her animal identity quickly, you may tape another animal to his or her back.

- Play continues until all students have guessed their animal identities.

Follow up–Encourage students in higher Stages to reflect on what language they used to describe the animals' regular activities (Present tense verbs).

Stages: ① — ② — ③ — ④ — ⑤

Extension

Academic Language Functions: Analyze

Grammar: Clauses with *because*

Students in Stages 4 and 5 can discuss what helped them or what caused them confusion in guessing the animal's identity with sentences, such as *I thought it was an owl because Inessa said it lives in trees.*

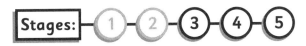

Stages: ① — ② — ③ — ④ — ⑤

Variation 1

Academic Language Function: Inquire

Grammar: *Wh-* questions; Yes/no questions with *Do/Am I...?*; Affirmative and negative short answers with *Yes, you do* or *No, you do not (don't)*; Contractions with *not*

Materials: Resource J: Animals

Students play the same guessing game as described in *Animal Facts*, but they get their clues by asking questions, such as *Where do I live?* or *Am I an amphibian?*

Follow up–Encourage students in higher Stages to reflect on what language they used to inquire about their animal identities (Questions).

Stages: ① — ② — ③ — ④ — ⑤

Variation 2

Academic Language Function: Describe

Grammar: Yes/no questions with *Is it...?*; Affirmative and negative short answers with *Yes, it is. No it's not* or *it isn't*

Materials: Resource J: Animals

Students guess an animal's identity in a similar manner as described in *Animal Facts*, but instead of circulating the room with the animal taped to their back, they sit in a circle with the animal above their heads, where they cannot see it.

- Arrange students in heterogeneous groups of mixed language abilities with four to five students each. Distribute two to three animals to each student face down, making sure that the student to the left cannot see the animals.

- Students take turns holding one animal above the head of the student to his or her left so that all the other students can see it. Students then offer the student clues about the animal, such as *It is a mammal* or *It lives in the forest.*

- If the student has not guessed the animal in a minute or two, the student holding the card shows the card to the student, and the game moves on, with the student who had been guessing now holding one of his or her cards above the student to his or her left.

Animal Action

Stages: 1 — 2 — 3 — 4 — 5

Academic Language Function: Describe

Grammar: Present continuous with *is* and *are*; Regular and irregular plurals; Quantity words *all, some, none*

Materials: Animal Habitats Scene

Groups of students describe the Animal Habitats Scene with as many sentences as they can in three minutes.

- Distribute one copy of the Animal Habitats Scene to heterogeneous groups of mixed language abilities with three to four students each.

- Students describe the scene with present continuous sentences, such as *A turtle is swimming* or *The geese are flying.* Encourage students in Stages 1 and 2 to point to the animals' activities and name them as they are able. Students in lower Stages can also be the ones to tally the number of sentences produced by their group.

- The group that has generated the most sentences in three minutes wins.

Follow up–Encourage students in higher Stages to reflect on what language they used to describe the animals' actions (present continuous tense).

Stages: 1 — 2 — 3 — 4 — 5

Variation 1

Academic Language Function: Describe

Grammar: Past continuous with *was* and *were*

Materials: Animal Habitats Scene

Groups study the Animal Habitats Scene for a minute or two, then turn the picture over and describe it in a game-like fashion as described in *Animal Action* with past continuous sentences, such as *A turtle was swimming* or *The geese were flying.*

Follow up–Encourage students in higher Stages to reflect on what language they used to describe the animals' actions that they saw going on (past continuous tense).

Stages: 1 — 2 — 3 — 4 — 5

Variation 2

Academic Language Function: Describe

Grammar: Clauses with *that;* Present continuous with *is* and *are;* Simple present tense verbs *is* and *are*

Materials: Animal Habitats Scene

Groups describe the picture in a game-like fashion as described in *Animal Action* using sentences with *that,* such as *The bird that is in the tree is singing* or *The bird that is gathering seeds is on the ground.*

Stages: 1 — 2 — 3 — 4 — 5

Animal Sort

Academic Language Functions: Classify, Solve problems, Evaluate; Compare and contrast

Social Language Function: Negotiate

Grammar: Compound sentences with *and* and *but;* Descriptive adjectives; Adverbs *too* and *also;* Comparative and superlative; Contractions with *is;* Suggestions with *Let's* or *How about...?;* Wh-questions with *Where* and *What;* Location words *here* and *there;* Demonstrative adjectives *this* and *that*

Materials: Resource J: Animals

Students sort Animal cards into categories.

- Make one copy of Resource J: Animals for each group.

- Arrange students into heterogeneous groups of mixed language abilities with three to four students each.

- Students cut out and then sort their animals into categories. Students should then discuss their categories with sentences, such as *The frog goes here because it's an amphibian* or *The squirrel goes here because it has fur,* and so on. Students in Stages 2 and 3 can discuss the categories with words or simple phrases, such as *here, big* or *here, fur.* Students in Stage 1 can participate by sorting and pointing, naming animals or qualities as they are able.

- Once all the cards are sorted, students in Stages 2–5 can compare their sorts with sentences, such as *These are mammals, but these are fish* or *There are more mammals than reptiles,* and so forth. Students in Stages 2 and 3 may use words or phrases, such as *Mammals, Fish* or *More mammals.*

Follow up–Encourage students in higher Stages to reflect on what language they used to compare and contrast the categories (Comparative with *more, less, fewer,* or other comparative words with *–er;* Compound sentences with *and* and *but*).

Which Animal?

Stages: 1 – 2 – 3 – 4 – 5

Academic Language Function: Describe

Grammar: Present continuous; Present tense verbs; Yes/no questions with *Is it...?* or *Does it...?;* Affirmative and negative short answers with *Yes, it is. No, it isn't or it's not. Yes, it does. No, it doesn't.;* Contractions with *not* and *is;* Prepositions–location

Materials: Animal Habitats Scene

Students guess which animal a group member is thinking of.

- Arrange students into groups of mixed language abilities with three to four students each.

- Make one copy of the Animal Habitats Scene for each group of students.

- Students take turns thinking of an animal in the scene without telling the other group members which one. The student then gives clues to the group about the animal with sentences, such as *It is gathering nuts* or *It is in the pond.* Group members guess after each clue by asking yes/no questions such as *Is it a squirrel?*

Follow up–Encourage students to reflect on what language they used to describe the animals' activities shown in the scene (Present continuous tense).

Stages: 1 - 2 - 3 - 4 - 5

Extension

Academic Language Function: Analyze

Grammar: Clauses with *because*

Students in higher Stages can explain how they knew or were confused by which animal was being described with sentences, such as *I thought Ibrahim was describing the turtle in the pond because... .*

Stages: 1 - 2 - 3 - 4 - 5

Variation 1

Academic Language Function: Inquire

Grammar: *Wh-* and yes/no questions; Affirmative and negative short answers with *Yes, it is. No, it's not* or *it isn't. Yes, it does. No, it doesn't;* Present tense verbs; Present continuous tense

Students ask questions to guess the animal that a group member is thinking of instead of the group member giving clues as described in *Which Animal?* Students in Stages 2–3 may use words or simple phrases, such as *in forest?*

Follow up–Encourage students in higher Stages to reflect on what language they used to inquire about the animals' activities.

Stages: 1 - 2 - 3 - 4 - 5

Variation 2

Academic Language Functions: Describe, Explain

Grammar: Infinitives, Gerunds

Students try to get their group to guess which animal they are thinking of by giving clues to each other about the animal's adaptive characteristics, using infinitives, such as *It has a shell to protect itself,* or gerunds, such as *It uses its wings for flying away.* Students in Stage 3 may use simple phrases, such as *shell to protect* or *wing for flying.*

Stages: 1 — 2 — 3 — **4** — **5**

Variation 3

Academic Language Functions: Describe, Compare and contrast

Grammar: Comparative, Adjectives, Adverbs

Materials: Animal Habitats Scene

Students try to get their group to guess which animal they are thinking of by giving clues to each other about the animal's characteristics using comparative forms, such as *It is bigger than the duck* or *It has more fur than the squirrel* or *It moves faster than a turtle.*

Follow up–Encourage students in higher Stages to reflect on what language they used to compare and contrast the animals' characteristics (*more, fewer, less,* adverbs and adjectives with *-er*).

Stages: **1** — **2** — **3** — **4** — **5**

Animal Life Cycle

Academic Language Function: Sequence

Social Language Functions: Agree and disagree, Negotiate

Grammar: Location words *here* and *there;* Helping verbs *should* and *ought to;* Prepositions–time; Sequence words, such as *first, next,* and *then*

Materials: Resource K: Animal Life Cycles
scissors, markers

Students arrange all the stages of the moth and/or frog life cycle in order.

- Make enough copies of Resource K: Animal Life Cycles to have one for each group.

- Arrange students into heterogeneous groups of mixed language abilities with three to four students each. Distribute the resource page to each group. Have students color and cut out the cards.

- Groups arrange the phases of the moth's and/or frog's life cycle in order using sentences, such as *The moth should go last because that's the end of its life cycle.* Students in Stage 3 may use simple phrases, such as *Moth last.* Students in Stages 1 and 2 may place the stages in order, naming them as they are able.

Follow up – Encourage students in higher Stages to reflect on what language they used to sequence (*First, next, then, after that, before, last*).

Animals Hide

Stages: 1 – 2 – 3 – 4 – 5

Academic Language Function: Explain

Grammar: Clauses with *because*

Materials: Animal Habitats Scene

Students color and discuss the Animal Habitats Scene, highlighting the features that provide some of the animals with camouflage.

- Make one copy of the Animal Habitats Scene for each student. Have students color their scenes, highlighting the animals' features that provide them with camouflage.

- Arrange students in heterogeneous groups of mixed language abilities with three to four students each. Have students explain their coloring using sentences with *because*, such as *I colored the turtle and the log brown because brown helps the turtle hide on the log.*

Follow up – Encourage students in higher Stages to reflect on what language they used to explain (*because*).

Memory

Academic Language Functions: Describe, Explain

Grammar: Clauses with *because;* Quantity word *both;* Irregular plural nouns

Materials: Resource J: Animals

Students try to match as many pairs of cards as they can.

- Make two copies of Resource J: Animals for each group.

- Arrange students in heterogeneous groups of mixed language abilities with three to four students each. Have students cut out the cards, mix them up, and arrange them face down in even rows.

- Students take turns turning over two cards at a time to see if they have a match. A match is made when two identical cards are turned over. Students in higher Stages should use language to describe their match. *This is a match because both are raccoons.* Students in Stages 2 and 3 may use words or simple phrases, such as *raccoons.* Students in Stage 1 may make matches, naming the animals as they are able.

- A player's turn continues as long as he/she continues to make matches. The player keeps the matches that he or she makes. If no match is made, the cards are turned back over, and the next player takes a turn.

- When all the cards have been matched, students count their matches. The person with the most matches wins.

Follow up–Encourage students in higher Stages to reflect on what language they used to explain their matches (*because*).

Go "Fish"

Stages: 1 — 2 — 3 — 4 — 5

Academic Language Functions: Inquire, Explain

Grammar: Yes/no questions with *Do you...?*; Affirmative and negative short answers with *Yes, I do. No, I don't;* Contractions with *not;* Quantity word *both*

Materials: Resource J: Animals

Students play "Go Fish" with the animal cards.

- Make two copies of Resource J: Animals for each group.

- Arrange students into heterogeneous groups of mixed language abilities with three to four students each. Distribute the two copies of Resource J: Animals to each group and have the group members cut out the cards. Have students shuffle the cards and distribute seven to each player. The remaining cards are spread out into a "pond."

- The players start by laying out any matching pairs they can make from their hand. Matches consist of two identical animal cards.

- Students then take turns asking any one person in the group a question, such as *Do you have a butterfly?* or *Do you have a frog?* to make a match with a card in their hand. Students in Stage 3 may use phrases, such as *Frog?* If the student has what was asked of him or her, he or she must give it to the player. The player lays down the pair, explaining the match with a sentence, such as *Both of these are squirrels.* Students in Stage 3 may explain with phrases, such as *Both raccoons.*

- If the student does not have what was asked for, he or she says *Go fish,* and the player must pick up a card from the "pond." If the player picks up a card that was asked for, he or she makes a match with the card in his or her hand, lays down the pair, and takes another turn.

- The first student who has no more cards in his or her hand is the winner.

***Follow up*–**Encourage students in higher Stages to reflect on what language they used to explain their match (*both*).

Wishful Thinking

Social Language Function: Wish and hope

Grammar: Conditional clauses with *if*; Helping verbs *would* and *could*

Materials: Resource J: Animals, scissors

Students imagine what it would be like to be a certain animal.

- Divide the class into groups of mixed language abilities with four to five students each.

- Distribute one copy of Resource J: Animals to each group. Have students cut out the cards, and lay them out, face up, in the middle of the group.

- Students take turns choosing an animal from the stack and stating that they wish they were that animal and what they would do if they were. For example, the first student to choose an animal says *I wish I were a bird. If I were a bird, I would fly around to my friends.* The next student needs to repeat what the first student said and add another conditional statement. For example, the second student says *If I were a bird, I would fly around to my friends, and I could live in a tree.* Play continues until all students in the group have added to the statements about the animal. At this point, the group starts over with the person who chose the card starting the next cycle of statements.

- If a student cannot remember what the others have said, he or she is out of the game. Keep in mind that each idea does not have to be perfectly stated.

- Play continues until there is only one student left—the winner.

Follow up—Encourage students to reflect on what language they used to express their wishes and what they would/could do if their wishes came true (*wish; If; would* and *could*)

My Favorite Animal

Academic Language Functions: Explain, Justify and persuade

Social Language Function: Agree and disagree

Grammar: Clauses with *because;* Affirmative and negative present tense verbs; Irregular past tense verb *drew;* Affirmative and negative helping verbs such as *could (not)* and *must (not);* Demonstrative pronouns/adjectives *this* and *that;* Adverb *probably*

Materials: Paper, markers or crayons

Students illustrate an animal they like. The class then plays a guessing game with the pictures.

- Students illustrate their favorite animal in its habitat without other students seeing. Make sure they *do not* put their name on their pictures.

- Display the drawings to the whole class and have students guess who drew which animal, explaining why they think so with sentences, such as *I think Christophe drew this because he loves snakes.* Students in Stage 3 may use simple phrases, such as *Christophe like snake.* Students in Stage 2 may name the classmate that they think drew the picture. Students in Stage 1 can participate by contributing drawings and naming a student as they are able.

- The class then engages in a discussion where students who don't agree argue their point, and where students who are sure of their guesses try to justify their position and persuade the other class members to agree.

- The student who drew the picture being discussed can then share his or her reason for drawing that particular animal as their favorite.

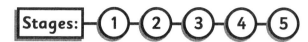

Home Culture Share 🌐

Academic Language Functions: Report, Explain

Grammar: Clauses with *where;* Present tense sentences with *There are*

Materials: paper, markers or crayons, scissors, map tacks, string, classroom world map

Students color an animal native to their home culture and share it with the class.

- Have students draw an animal native to their family's home culture. Put the pictures around a classroom world map. Use string and map tacks to connect the animal with its natural habitat.

- Once all the animals are around the map, have students report to the class by explaining some things about that animal and its habitat with sentences, such as *There are deserts where my family is from, and that's where scorpions live.* Students in Stage 3 may use phrases to explain, such as *This scorpion. Live desert.* Students in Stages 1 and 2 may simply point, naming the animal and its habitat as they are able.

***Follow up*–**Encourage students in higher Stages to reflect on what language they used to explain the animals' habitats (*where* and *live*).

Home-School Connection

Academic Language Functions: Report, Explain

Students color the Animal Habitats Scene and describe it to someone at home. They should describe it first in English, and then discuss it in either English or their home language.

Plants

Content Area Vocabulary

acorn	garden	seed
beanstalk	grass	seedling
berry	grow	soil
branch	leaf/leaves	sprout
bud	milkweed	stem
bulb	moss	sunflower
bush	oak/maple/	sunlight
corn	apple/pine tree	tomato
daisy	pepper	tree
dandelion	petal	trunk
fern	pine cones	tulip
field	plant	vine
flower	pod	water
food	reproduce	wheat
fruit	root	

Before beginning, make sure your students are familiar with the content area vocabulary, functions, and grammar points necessary for engaging in each activity. The activities in this unit offer students opportunities to practice language and content for which they have already received instruction. Assess students' participation in the activities and review as needed. Alternatively, you can use the activities to assess students' prior knowledge of the language functions and grammar points before teaching them. The information you collect can be used to guide your instruction.

Go "Fish"

Academic Language Functions: Inquire, Explain

Grammar: Present tense verbs; Yes/no questions with *Do you...?*; Affirmative and negative short answers with *Yes, I do* or *No I do not (don't)*; Contractions with *not*

Materials: Resource N: Plant Parts
scissors, markers

Students use the Plant Parts in a game of Go "Fish" as they try to assemble complete sunflower plants.

- Arrange students into heterogeneous groups of mixed language abilities with three to four students each.

- Give each group one fewer Resource N: Plant Parts than the number of students in the group. For example, if a group has four students, provide three copies. Have students color and cut out the cards. One student in the group should then hand out three cards to each player in an alternating fashion. Students should use books or folders to set up a barrier so that other students can not see their cards. The remaining cards should be placed face down between the players.

- Students look at their plant cards without letting the other players see them. As in the game Go "Fish," they then take turns asking other players for the Plant Parts they need to complete the sunflower plant. For example, students can ask *Do you have roots?* Students in lower Stages may use phrases or single words, such as *roots?*

- If the player has the card being requested, he or she asks the other player why that card is needed. The other player responds by explaining the importance of the particular Plant Part requested. Students in Stages 4-5 should reply in complete sentences, such as *Roots help plants get water.* Students in Stage 3 may say *roots for water.* The player gives the requested card to the other student, and he or she must discard one card.

- If the player does not have the card being requested, he or she should say "Go Fish" (or another phrase of your choosing), and the player requesting the card takes one from the pile. If the player pulls the card that was requested, he or she gets to go again.

- The first player to construct a complete sunflower plant wins.

Follow up–Encourage students in higher Stages to reflect on what language they used to inquire (*Do you have...?*).

Stages: 1 - 2 - ③ - ④ - ⑤

Variation 1

Academic Language Functions: Inquire, Explain

Grammar: Present tense verbs; Yes/no questions with *Do you...?*; Affirmative and negative short answers with *Yes, I do* or *No, I do not (don't)*; Contractions with *not*; Infinitives

Materials: Resource N: Plant Life Cycle

Play proceeds as described in *Go "Fish,"* but instead of trying to get all the parts of a sunflower, students try to get all the stages of a plant's life cycle.

- In this variation, when players are asked why they need the card, they may respond with sentences, such as *I need the seedling to come out of the ground* or *I need the pods to reproduce.*

Stages: ① - ② - ③ - ④ - ⑤

Match the Plants

Academic Language Function: Describe

Social Language Function: Agree and disagree

Grammar: Demonstrative pronouns *This* and *These*; Present tense verbs; Quantity word *both*; Present tense sentences with *These are...*

Materials: Resource L: Plants

Students play a game of "Memory" with the Plants cards.

- Copy and cut out two copies of Resource L: Plants for each group.

- Arrange students in heterogeneous groups of mixed language abilities with three to four students each. Distribute two sets of the Plants cards to each group. Have students color and cut out the cards. They should then mix the cards up and arrange them upside down in even rows.

- Students should then take turns turning over two cards at a time, trying to make a match. If a student can make a justifiable connection between two cards, they are considered a match. For example, a student may say *These two go together because they are trees* or *These go together because they both have leaves*. Students in Stage 3 may use phrases, such as *both trees*. Students in Stages 1 and 2 may make matches, naming them as they are able.

- If a student makes a match, he or she may then take another turn. If not, play goes on to the next group member.

- The student with the most matches at the end of the game wins.

Follow up–Encourage students in higher Stages to reflect on what language they used to compare (*both*).

Describe the Scene

Stages: 1 – 2 – 3 – 4 – 5

Academic Language Functions: Express position, Describe

Grammar: Prepositions–location; Present tense sentences with *There is/ There are*

Materials: Farmer's Garden Scene

Groups of students describe the Farmer's Garden Scene with as many sentences as they can in three minutes.

- Distribute one copy of the Farmer's Garden Scene to heterogeneous groups of mixed language abilities with three to four students each.

- Students describe the picture using sentences, such as *There is a tree behind the bush* or *There is a flower in the garden*. Students in Stage 3 may use phrases such as *tree behind bush* or *flower in garden*. Students in Stages 1 and 2 can point to plants, naming them as they are able. Students in lower Stages can also tally the number of sentences produced by the group.

- The group that has generated the most sentences in three minutes wins.

Follow up–Encourage students in higher Stages to reflect on what language they used to describe the scene and express the position of plants (*There is/are;* prepositions).

Stages: 1–2–3–4–5

Variation 1

Academic Language Function: Describe

Grammar: Past tense sentences with *There was/There were*

Materials: Farmer's Garden Scene

Groups study the Farmer's Garden Scene for a minute or two, then turn the picture over and describe it using past tense sentences with *There was.../There were...* .

Stages: 1–2–3–4–5

Where Are You?

Academic Language Functions: Inquire, Express position

Grammar: Yes/ no questions with *Are you/ Is it?;* Affirmative and negative short answers with *Yes, I am, No I am (I'm) not* or *Yes, it is, No, it is (it's) not/it isn't;* Prepositions–location; Descriptive adjectives; Location words *here* and *there;* Contractions with *am, is,* and *not*

Materials: Farmer's Garden Scene
Resource A: People Manipulatives

Students guess their partners' location in the Farmer's Garden Scene.

- Arrange students in pairs and distribute one copy of Resource A: People Manipulatives and the Farmer's Garden Scene to each student. Have students color and cut out a "self" manipulative. Arrange the pairs back-to-back so that they cannot see each other's scenes.

- Students take turns placing themselves in the scene. Partners should then ask questions to guess the student's location. For example, they might ask *Are you near a tree? Is it a big tree?* Students in Stage 3 can use phrases, such as *near tree? big tree?* When the partner thinks that he or she has guessed the correct location, the student should show his or her placement in the scene.

Follow up–Encourage students in higher Stages to reflect on what language they used to inquire (*Are you/Is it...?*).

Stages: 1 — 2 — 3 — **4** — **5**

Extension

Academic Language Function: Analyze

Grammar: Clauses with *because*

Students in higher Stages can discuss what helped or hindered their guessing the correct placement with sentences, such as *I thought you were here because you said you were next to a bush.*

Stages: 1 — 2 — **3** — **4** — **5**

Variation 1

Academic Language Functions: Inquire, Express position

Grammar: Yes/no questions with *Is he/she...* or *Are they...?*; Affirmative and negative short answers with *Yes, he/she is, No, he/she is not* (or *he's/she's not* or *he/she isn't*), *Yes they are* or *No, they are not* or *they're not* or *they aren't*; Contractions with *is, not,* and *are*; Preposition–location

Materials: Farmer's Garden Scene
　　　　　　Resource A: People Manipulatives
　　　　　　Resource J: Animals

Each student takes a turn placing one or several of the People Manipulatives or Animals on the scene. The student should tell his or her partner which cards are being placed on the scene. Then the partner asks questions to determine where the cards are placed. For example, a partner might ask, *Is the boy in the garden? Is he near the corn?* or *Is the mouse in a tree?* and so on. Students in Stage 3 may use phrases, such as *Near tree? Big tree?* Have students show their pictures and discuss the placements, people, and animals as described in *Where Are You?* Have students in Stages 4–5 discuss their successes and discrepancies in placement as described in the Extension above.

***Follow up*–**Encourage students in higher Stages to reflect on what language they used to express position (*near, in,* and so on).

Stages: 1 — 2 — 3 — 4 — 5

Variation 2

Academic Language Functions: Describe, Express position

Grammar: Present tense verbs *am* and *is;* Prepositions–location

Materials: Resource A: People Manipulatives or
Resource J: Animals
Farmer's Garden Scene

Based on clues their partner gives them, students guess the placement of one of the People Manipulatives or Animals in the Farmer's Garden Scene. For example, the partner might say *A boy is in the garden. He is next to a fruit tree* or *A raccoon is in the woods. It is in a tree,* and so on. Students in Stage 3 may use phrases as described in *Where Are You?*. Have students show their pictures and discuss the placements as described in the previous variation. Students in Stages 4–5 should discuss their successes and discrepancies in placement as described in the Extension activity on page 136.

Stages: 1 — 2 — 3 — 4 — 5

Variation 3

Academic Language Function: Express position

Social Language Function: Give instructions

Grammar: Commands; Prepositions–location

Materials: Resource A: People Manipulatives or
Resource J: Animals
Farmer's Garden Scene

Have one student in each pair place some or all of the people/animals in the scene without his or her partner seeing. Partners follow the students' directions in placing the

People Manipulatives or Animals on the scene in the same places. For example, a student may say *Put the woman next to the flowers* or *Put the snake in the grass.* Students in Stage 3 may use phrases as described in *Where Are You.* Students in Stage 2 may participate by following their partners' directions. Once the student is finished directing his or her partner, have them compare their pictures and discuss the placements as described in *Where Are You?.*

● Have students in Stages 4–5 discuss their successes and discrepancies in placement as described in the Extension activity.

Follow up–Encourage students in higher Stages to reflect on what language they used to give instructions (*Put*).

Home-School Connection

Academic Language Functions: Report, Describe

Have students color and bring home a copy of the Farmer's Garden Scene and describe it to someone at home. They should describe the scene first in English and then discuss it in either English or their home language.

What Is It?

Stages: 1 — 2 — 3 — 4 — 5

Academic Language Function: Inquire

Social Language Function: Agree and disagree

Grammar: Yes/no questions with *Is it...?* or *Does it have...?*; Affirmative and negative short answers with *Yes, it is. No, It is (it's) not* (or *isn't*). *Yes, it does, No, it does not (doesn't)*; Contractions with *is* and *not*; Affirmative and negative present tense verbs

Materials: Farmer's Garden Scene

Students guess a group member's choice of plant in the Farmer's Garden Scene.

- Arrange students in heterogeneous groups of mixed language abilities of three to four students each.

- Distribute one or more copies of Farmer's Garden Scene to each group.

- One student chooses a plant from the Farmer's Garden Scene without telling the other group members which one. The other group members then ask yes/no questions, such as *Does it have a trunk?* or *Is it a vegetable?* to guess the plant. Students in Stages 2–3 may use words or phrases, such as *Have trunk?, Vegetable?* Students in Stage 1 may participate by using gestures, such as nodding or pointing, or naming the items as they are able.

- When one group member thinks he or she knows the student's chosen plant, he or she names the plant and points to it in the scene. The student who is thinking of the plant should remain silent at this point. Group members then discuss whether they agree or disagree. Discussion continues until the group members come to a consensus. The student should then share which plant he or she was actually thinking of.

Follow up–Encourage students in higher Stages to reflect on what language they used to agree and disagree (*I don't think so because...*).

Stages: 1 – 2 – 3 – 4 – 5

Extension

Academic Language Functions: Analyze

Grammar: Clauses with *because*

Encourage students in Stages 4–5 to reflect on what helped or hindered their guessing the plant that the student was thinking of with sentences, such as *I thought it was this flower because Ferdous said it had buds on it.*

Variation 1

Academic Language Function: Describe

Social Language Function: Agree and disagree

Grammar: Descriptive adjectives; Affirmative and negative present tense verbs *has, have,* and *is*; Contractions with *not* and *is*

Materials: Farmer's Garden Scene

In this variation, group members take turns choosing different types of plants in the scene and describing them until the other group members guess which plant. For example, a student might say *It doesn't have any flowers* or *It is (It's) small,* and so on. Play should proceed as described in *What Is It?* with group members discussing and deciding which plant they think it is.

Follow up–Encourage students in higher Stages to reflect on what language they used to agree and disagree (affirmative and negative present tense verbs).

Put It Together

Academic Language Functions: Analyze, Inquire, Sequence, Express position, Compare and contrast, Evaluate, Explain, Justify and persuade, Solve problems, Report

Social Language Functions: Agree and disagree, Express obligation, Give instructions, Negotiate

Grammar: Commands; Sequence words; *Wh-* questions with *where;* Helping verbs such as *should;* Suggestions such as *Let's...*, *How about...?*, and *Why don't we...?*

Materials: Resource M: Plant Life Cycles

Students work together to identify and describe the stages of the plant life cycle.

- Arrange students into heterogeneous groups of mixed language abilities with three to four students each. Distribute one copy of Resource M: Plant Life Cycles to each group.

- Have students color and cut out the cards and line them up in random order.

- Have students discuss the placement of cards to create a plant life cycle. For example, a student may start the discussion by asking *What goes first?* Another student may say *I think we should put plant with pods first.* Another student may disagree, and so forth. Students in Stages 2 and 3 may use words and phrases, such as *What first?* and *plant with seeds.* Students in Stage 1 may participate by using gestures, such as placing the cards and pointing and/or naming the stages of the plant life cycle as they are able.

- Discussion continues until all the cards are placed into a plant life cycle.

- Groups should then share their plant life cycles with the class, comparing and contrasting them.

***Follow up*–**Encourage students in higher Stages to reflect on what language they used to suggest (*Let's...*, *How about...?*, *Why don't we...?*).

Stages: — ① – ② – ③ – ④ – ⑤

Variation 1

Academic Language Functions: Sequence, Express position

Social Language Function: Give instructions

Grammar: Commands; Sequence words, such as *first, next, then, before, after,* and so on

Materials: Resource M: Plant Life Cycles and an overhead projector

Students direct the teacher as he/she places the different stages of the plant life cycle in the correct order using an overhead projector.

- Make a copy of Resource M: Plant Life Cycles on a transparency and cut out the parts.

- Arrange the cut out pictures in random order on the overhead projector screen.

- Invite students to help you place the pictures in the correct growth order using sentences, such as *First, there is a plant with pods. Next, a seed falls to the ground* and so on.

- Students in Stages 2 or 3 can direct you with words or phrases, such as *seed first* or *sprouting seed next*. Stage 1 students may participate by watching and listening, and naming the items to be placed as they are able.

Follow up–Encourage students in higher Stages to reflect on what language they used to sequence (*first, next, then,* and so on).

Which Plant Scene?

Stages: 1 - 2 - 3 - 4 - 5

Academic Language Functions: Describe

Grammar: Present tense sentences with *There is/there are*; Quantity words; Prepositions–location; Possessives with *'s*; Subject pronoun *one*; Demonstrative adjectives *this* and *that*; Helping verbs, such as *may, might, could,* and *must*; Possessive pronouns *his/hers*; Clauses with *because*

Materials: Drawing paper and markers

Students use self-drawn scenes containing plants.

- Invite students to draw their own plants scene. Do not dictate what plants to use or where to put them. Encourage each student to choose one plant setting to draw, such as a mountain, a forest, a vegetable garden, an orchard, or the desert. Make sure each student puts their name on the front of their picture, or you can write it for those who are not yet able to do so.

- Tell students that their pictures should include things that plants need in order to grow.

- Once students have drawn their scenes, gather the class together and put all of the students' pictures on a table or display them on a bulletin board. Model the activity by describing one of the pictures yourself without indicating which one you are describing. Use sentences, such as *There are four trees* or *There are some flowers next to a bush.*

- Invite students to guess which picture you are describing. For example, a student might say *I think it's this one* or *It could be Maria's picture because hers has flowers*. Students in Stage 3 may use phrases, such as *this one* or *Maria's because flowers*. Students in Stages 1 and 2 can participate by pointing, naming the pictures as they are able with words or phrases, such as *This* or *Maria*.

- Invite students in Stages 3–5 to describe other pictures on the table for their classmates to guess.

Follow up–Encourage students in higher Stages to reflect on what language was used to give reasons (clauses with *because*).

Match the Foods

Stages: (1)-(2)-(3)-(4)-(5)

Academic Language Functions: Classify, Describe, Evaluate, Explain, Express position, Inquire, Justify and persuade, Solve problems, Report

Social Language Functions: Agree and disagree, Express obligation, Give instructions, Negotiate

Grammar: Helping verbs *should, must* and *has to*; Affirmative and negative present tense verbs; Past tense verbs; Clauses with *because* and *so*; Location words *here* and *there*; Suggestions with *Let's*; Wh-questions with *Where...?*; Negative statements with *can*

Materials: Farmer's Garden Scene
Resource E: Foods

Students match foods to the Farmer's Garden Scene.

- Make enough copies of Resource E: Foods and the Farmer's Garden Scene for each group.

- Arrange students into heterogeneous groups of mixed language abilities with three to four students each. Have students cut out the food cards and spread them out.

- Students should then place the Food cards on the Farmer's Garden Scene as they see fit. For example, a student may start by taking one card and asking *Where should we put milk?* Another student may say I *think we should put it with sheep. Sheep produce milk* and so on. Students in Stage 3 may use phrases, such as *Where milk?* and *Milk sheep.* Students in Stages 1 and 2 may place cards, naming them as they are able.

- Students will not be able to include all of the Foods cards on the Farmer's Garden Scene. This will give them practice with negative sentences, such as *We can't put bananas on the scene because there is not a banana tree.*

- Once groups have sorted through all of their Foods cards, Stage 4 or 5 students from the groups should share their placements with the class with explanations, such as *We put tortillas with the corn because they are made from corn.*

Follow up–Encourage students in higher Stages to reflect on what language they used to justify and persuade (*must*).

Sort the Plants

Academic Language Functions: Classify, Describe, Evaluate, Explain, Express position, Inquire, Justify and persuade, Solve problems, Report

Social Language Functions: Agree and disagree, Express obligation, Give instructions, Negotiate

Grammar: Affirmative and negative present tense verbs; Present tense sentences with *This is*; Suggestions with *Let's*; Present tense verbs *be* and *have*; Helping verb *should*; Coordinating conjunction *or*

Materials: Resource L: Plants

Students sort the Plants cards into categories.

- Copy and cut out Resource A: Plants so that you have one set for each group.

- Arrange students into heterogeneous groups of mixed language abilities with three to four students each. Distribute one set of cards to each group.

- Have students spread out and sort through the cards, categorizing them as they go. For example, one student may say *This is a flower. Let's start a flower pile.* The next student may say *This is a bush. Should we put it with the trees or start a bush pile?* and so on.

- Once groups have sorted all their Plants cards, they should share their categories with the class.

Follow up–Encourage students in higher Stages to reflect on what language was used to classify.

Resource A: People/Transportation Manipulatives

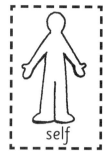
self

baby

boy

girl

woman

man

Note: Transportation manipulatives may be photocopied on an overhead transparency. That way students can flip the manipulatives to face the right direction.

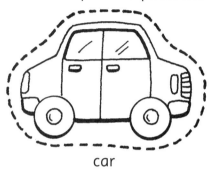
car

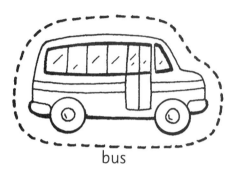
bus

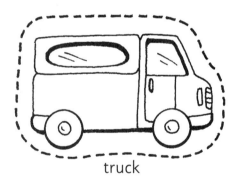
truck

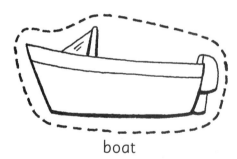
boat

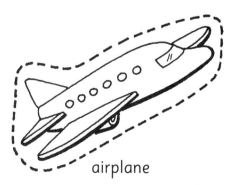
airplane

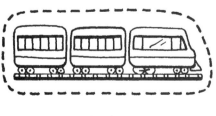
train

Resource B: Geography Spinner

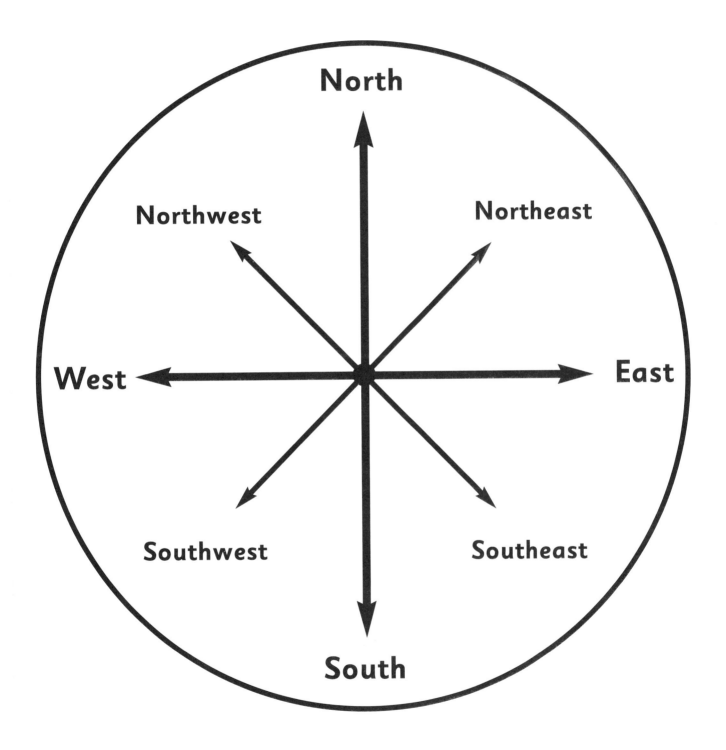

Resource C: Technology Items (Part One)

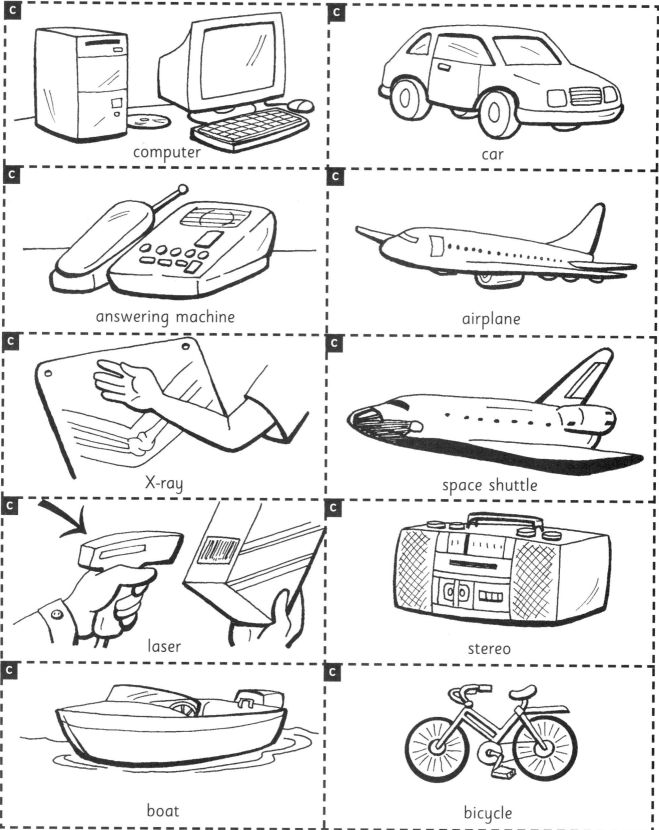

computer

car

answering machine

airplane

X-ray

space shuttle

laser

stereo

boat

bicycle

Resource C: Technology Items (Part Two)

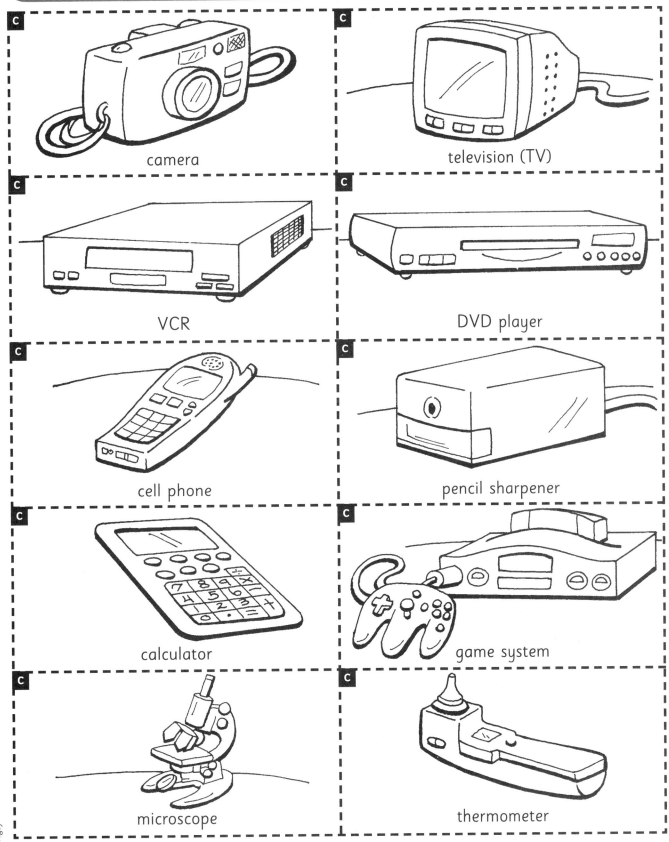

camera

television (TV)

VCR

DVD player

cell phone

pencil sharpener

calculator

game system

microscope

thermometer

Resource D: Technology Accessories

film	cassette	video
DVD	CD	CD ROM
satellite dish	bar code	phone number
pencil	math problem	remote control

Resource E: Foods (Part One)

spinach	milk	cheese	egg
fish	beans	green beans	chicken
corn	yam	potato	peppers
onion	banana	orange	mango
rice	tortilla	noodles	cereal

Resource E: Foods (Part Two)

candy	apple	pork	grapes
berries	beef	melon	oil
yogurt	nuts	lamb	carrot
eggplant	cucumber	cabbage	squash
bread	crackers	honey	lettuce

Resource F: Exercises

bike

walk

run

swim

jumping jacks

sit ups

pull ups

push ups

yoga

martial arts

softball

soccer

football

badminton

canoe

climb

dance

rollerblade

basketball

hockey

Resource G: Emergencies

fire

injury

tornado

break in

accident

heat wave

earthquake

snowstorm

rainstorm

flood

faint

sandstorm

car accident

hurricane

electricity off

water off

Resource H: Safety Devices

smoke alarm	helmet	knee & elbow pads	adult
fire extinguisher	hat	oven mitt	first aid kit
life jacket	jacket	flashlight	help sign
sunscreen	cell phone	seat belt	TV
radio	fire department	ambulance	police department

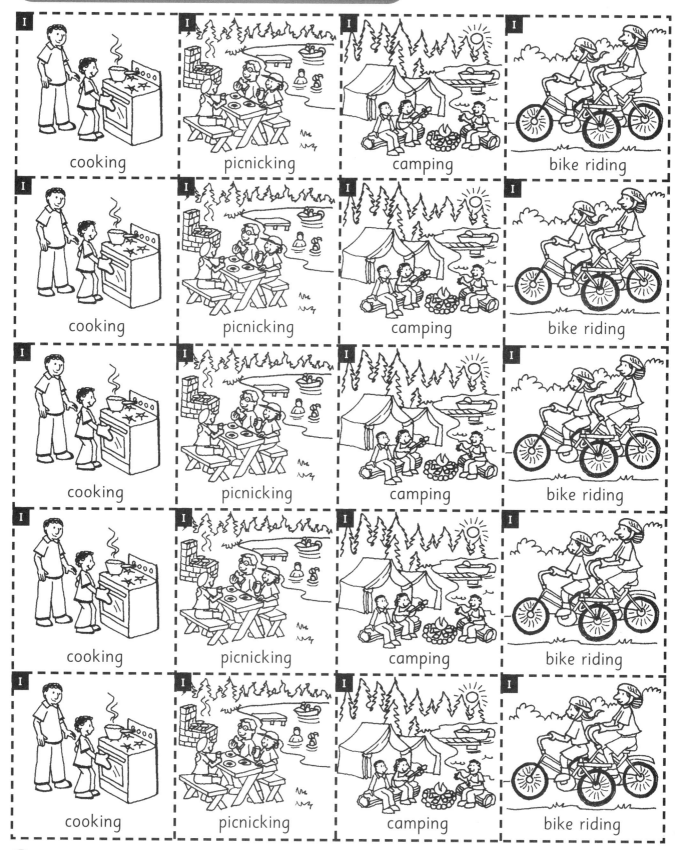

cooking   picnicking   camping   bike riding

cooking   picnicking   camping   bike riding

cooking   picnicking   camping   bike riding

cooking   picnicking   camping   bike riding

cooking   picnicking   camping   bike riding

Resource J: Animals

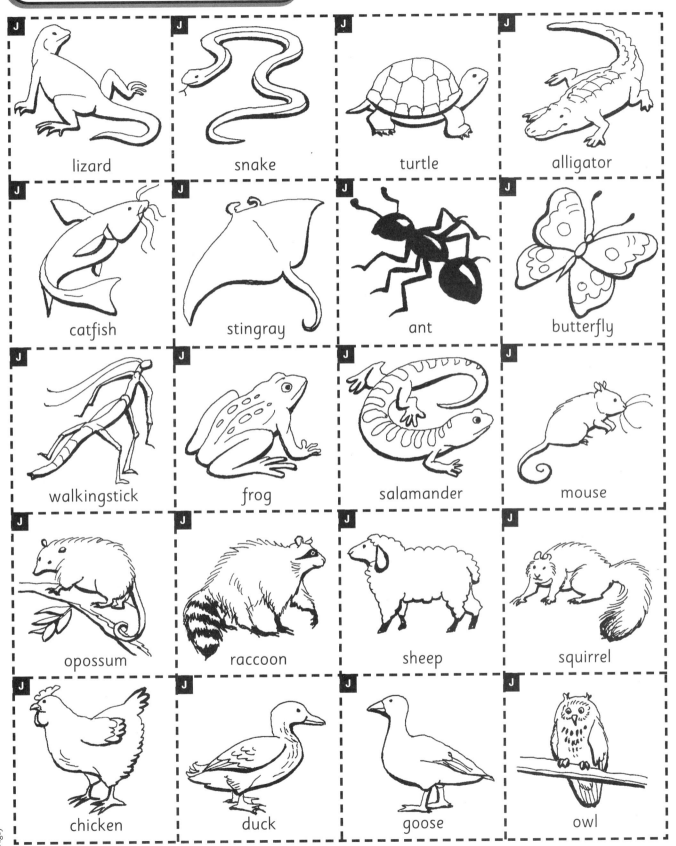

lizard	snake	turtle	alligator
catfish	stingray	ant	butterfly
walkingstick	frog	salamander	mouse
opossum	raccoon	sheep	squirrel
chicken	duck	goose	owl

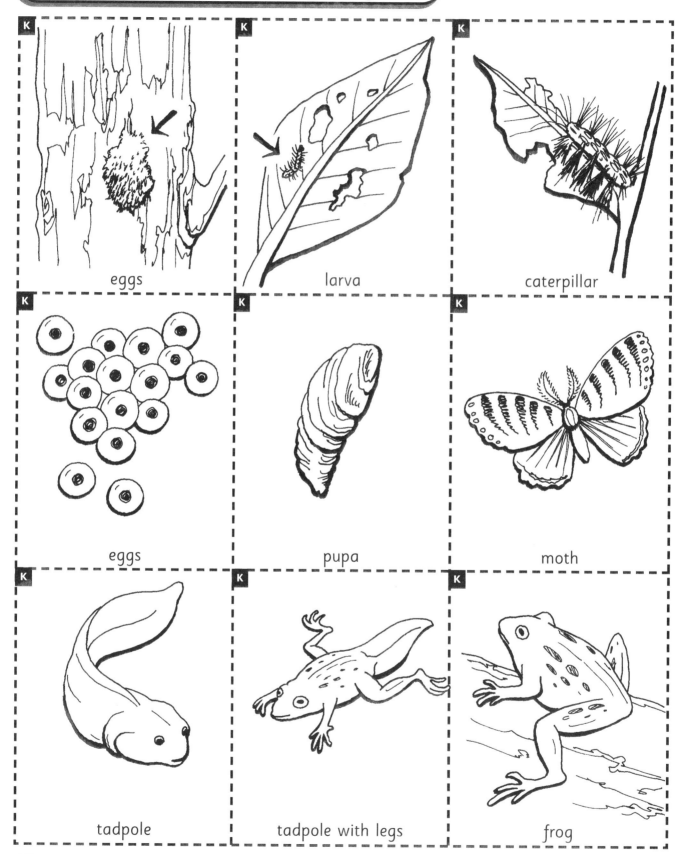

eggs

larva

caterpillar

eggs

pupa

moth

tadpole

tadpole with legs

frog

Rigby Best Teachers Press

© 2004 Rigby

Resource L: Plants

tulip

sunflower

bush

oak tree

maple tree

apple tree

pine tree

dandelion

milkweed

bean stalk

tomato vine

daisy

Resource M: Plant Life Cycles

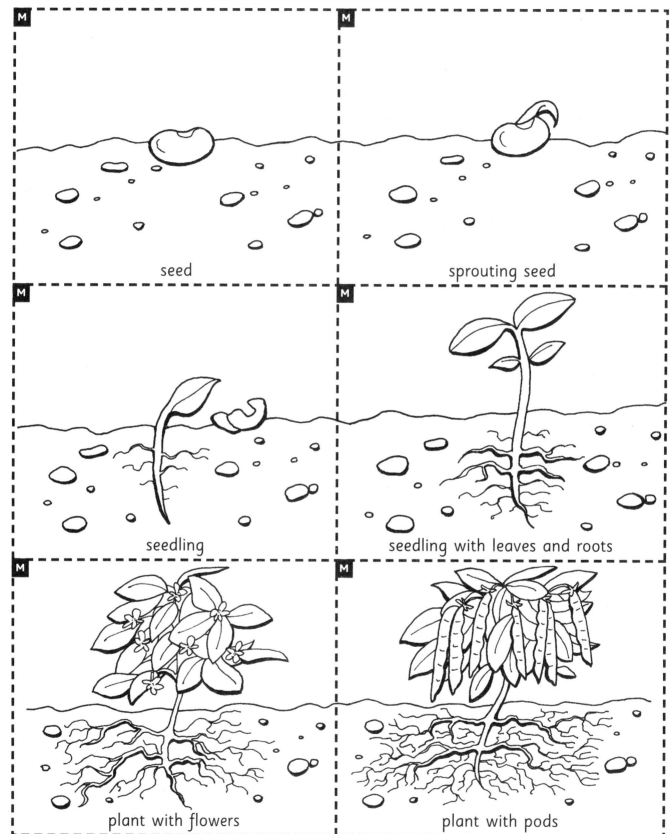

seed

sprouting seed

seedling

seedling with leaves and roots

plant with flowers

plant with pods

Resource N: Plant Parts

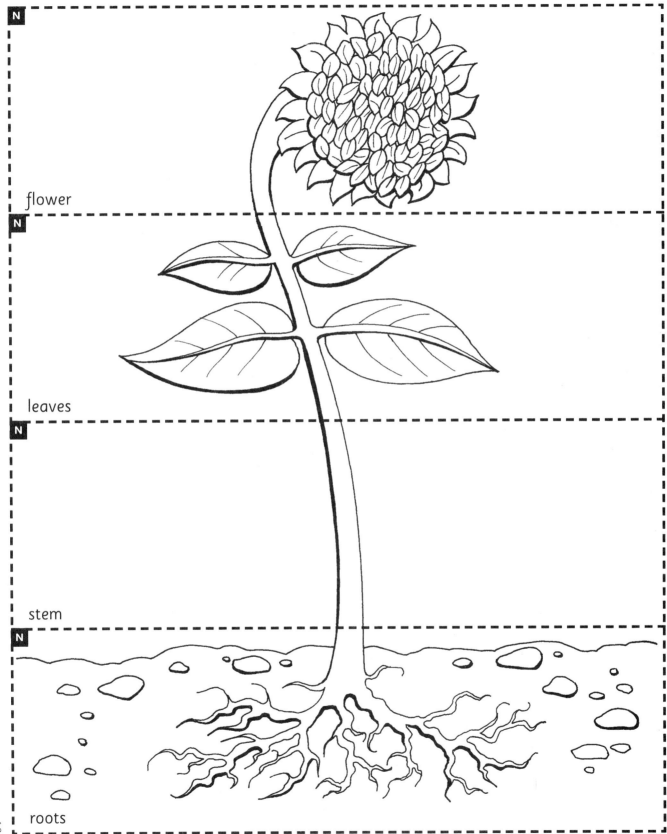

flower

leaves

stem

roots

Academic Language Functions Assessment

Student: _____   Date: _____

Activity: _____   Page: _____

Instructions: Put a check mark next to the academic language function you choose to assess. Observe the student during the activity, noting the student's oral language production. Assess his or her academic language proficiency using the grid below. This assessment can be placed in the student's portfolio and used to track his or her oral language performance.

Academic Language Functions:

☐ Analyze ☐ Classify ☐ Compare and contrast ☐ Describe ☐ Evaluate

☐ Explain ☐ Express position ☐ Inquire ☐ Justify and persuade ☐ Predict and hypothesize

☐ Report ☐ Sequence ☐ Solve problems ☐ Synthesize

Stage 1: Preproduction	Stage 2: Early Production	Stage 3: Speech Emergence	Stage 4: Intermediate Fluency	Stage 5: Advanced Fluency
Produces little, if any, spoken language, possibly gesturing or pointing to express language function	Uses some basic words and simple phrases related to the language function	Produces longer, complete phrases and possibly some sentences related to the language function	Uses complex sentences related to the language function; errors do not hinder communication	Speech related to the language function appears to be fluent and effortless, approximating that of native-speaking peers

Stage of Language Acquisition displayed during the activity: _____

Notes: _____

_____

_____

_____

Follow-up instruction: _____

_____

_____

_____

_____

Social Language Functions Assessment

Student: _____ Date: _____

Activity: _____ Page: _____

Instructions: Put a check mark next to the social language function you choose to assess. Observe the student during the activity, noting the student's oral language production. Assess his or her social language proficiency using the grid below. This assessment can be placed in the student's portfolio and used to track his or her oral language performance.

Social Language Functions:

☐ Agree and disagree   ☐ Apologize   ☐ Ask for assistance or permission

☐ Express feelings and needs   ☐ Express likes and dislikes   ☐ Express obligation

☐ Give instructions   ☐ Greet   ☐ Negotiate

☐ Use appropriate register   ☐ Use social etiquette   ☐ Warn   ☐ Wish and hope

Stage 1: Preproduction	Stage 2: Early Production	Stage 3: Speech Emergence	Stage 4: Intermediate Fluency	Stage 5: Advanced Fluency
Produces little, if any, spoken language, possibly gesturing or pointing to express language function	Uses some basic words and simple phrases related to the language function	Produces longer, complete phrases and possibly some sentences related to the language function	Uses complex sentences related to the language function; errors do not hinder communication	Speech related to the language function appears to be fluent and effortless, approximating that of native-speaking peers

Stage of Language Acquisition displayed during the activity: _____

Notes: _____

_____

_____

_____

Follow-up instruction: _____

_____

_____

_____

Grammar Usage Assessment

Student: _____ Date: _____

Activity: _____ Page: _____

Instructions: Put a check mark next to the grammar point(s) you choose to assess. Observe a student during the activity, noting the student's oral language during the activity. Assess his or her proficiency using the grammar point(s). Use the grid below to help you assess the student's performance. This assessment can be placed in the student's portfolio and used to track his or her language performance.

Grammar Points:

☐ Adjectives ☐ Adverbs ☐ Clauses ☐ Commands
☐ Comparative/Superlative ☐ Coordinating conjunctions ☐ Contractions ☐ Gerunds
☐ Helping verbs ☐ Infinitives ☐ Location words ☐ Negative
☐ Nouns ☐ Possessives ☐ Prepositional phrases ☐ Pronouns
☐ Quantity words ☐ Questions ☐ Sequence words ☐ Short answers
☐ Suggestions ☐ Verbs

Stage 1: Preproduction	Stage 2: Early Production	Stage 3: Speech Emergence	Stage 4: Intermediate Fluency	Stage 5: Advanced Fluency
Produces little, if any, spoken language, sometimes gesturing or pointing to the actions/situations/descriptions	Usually, points to actions/ situations/ descriptions, sometimes naming them	Uses phrases and simple sentences to express actions/ situations/ descriptions	States actions/ situations/ descriptions, using sentences with some errors that do not hinder communication	States actions/ situations/ descriptions fluently and effortlessly as would a native-speaking peer

Stage of Language Acquisition displayed during the activity: _____

Notes (Include details on the grammar point. For example, for *Verbs,* note which tense): _____

_____

_____

_____

Follow-up instruction: _____

_____

_____

_____

Content Area Vocabulary Assessment

Student: _____   Date: _____

Activity: _____   Page: _____

Instructions: Write the content area words you expect students to use in the chosen activity. Observe the student during the activity, noting the student's oral vocabulary use during the activity. Assess his or her proficiency using the content area vocabulary. Use the grid below to help you assess the student's performance. This assessment can be placed in the student's portfolio and used to track his or her oral language performance.

Content Area Vocabulary Words:

_____

_____

_____

Stage 1: Preproduction	Stage 2: Early Production	Stage 3: Speech Emergence	Stage 4: Intermediate Fluency	Stage 5: Advanced Fluency
Sometimes points to items when prompted	Usually points to items when prompted, sometimes naming them	Names key vocabulary items, usually using simple phrases or sentence patterns, such as *This mountain*	Uses key vocabulary in fluent discourse with some errors that do not impede meaning	Uses key vocabulary in fluent discourse, similar to that of native-speaking peers

Stage of Language Acquisition displayed during the activity: _____

Notes: _____

_____

_____

_____

Follow-up instruction: _____

_____

_____

_____

APPENDIX

Index

Index

Bibliography

Bloom, B.S. (Ed.) (1956). *Taxonomy of educational objectives: The classification of educational goals: Handbook I, cognitive domain.* New York; Toronto: Longmans, Green.

Cary, S. (1997). *Second language learners.* New York: Stenhouse Publishers.

Chamot, A. U. & O'Malley J. M.. (1994). *The CALLA handbook.* Addison-Wesley Publishing Company.

Gibbons, P. (1991). *Learning to learn in a second language.* Portsmouth, VA: Heinemann.

Peregoy, S. F. & Boyle O. F. (1997). *Reading, writing, and learning in ESL.* White Plains, NY: Longman.

Teachers of English to Speakers of Other Languages. (1997). *ESL standards for pre-K-12 students.* Teachers of English to Speakers of Other Languages, Inc.